Get Rich Now on A Secret Multi-Trillion Dollar Market

Trade Money, *Not* Stock

You can double your investment every month, almost automatically.

by S. G. Samuels

iUniverse, Inc.
New York   Bloomington

iUniverse books may be ordered through booksellers or by contacting:

iUniverse
1663 Liberty Drive
Bloomington, IN 47403
www.iuniverse.com
1-800-Authors (1-800-288-4677)

Because of the dynamic nature of the Internet, any Web addresses or links
contained in this book may have changed since publication and may no longer be
valid. The views expressed in this work are solely those of the author and do not
necessarily reflect the views of the publisher, and the publisher hereby disclaims
any responsibility for them.

ISBN: 978-1-4502-0162-9 (sc)
ISBN: 978-1-4502-0163-6 (ebook)
ISBN: 978-1-4502-0164-3 (hc)

Library of Congress Control Number: 2010900208

Printed in the United States of America

iUniverse rev. date: 01/19/2010

Contents

Dedication:

This book is dedicated to Lillian, Victor, Lewis, Philip and Lee Samuels for their patience and support while I worked tirelessly to 'crack' the forex code and turn this knowledge into your guide.

It is also dedicated to each of you who take the time to study it carefully and put it to good use.

Foreword:

First I want to thank you for purchasing this book to ensure your future of potential increased wealth and financial independence—in a market that you probably didn't even know existed. It's called the foreign money exchange (forex), and trillions of dollars are traded on this market daily. You may have thought the slow-moving, turtle-like stock market was big, but this is much bigger.

By the way, I set a goal of keeping this book as short and focused as possible so you can read through it more than once and begin to use this information to your own financial potential as quickly as possible. Although it could be a three hundred page topic, I'm taking a minimalistic approach, providing you the most important insider information on the forex market with brevity.

What makes this market so exciting to me is that after traveling the globe and constantly exchanging money at those money-exchange booths at airports (forex traders), I realized that there must be a much bigger trading market and system. Think about companies that import and export goods internationally on a daily basis; they issue purchase orders and then are invoiced by the supplier, and they have to pay for the goods. How do they do this? Usually they will ask their bank to help them wire the money, but to do so it has to go through a conversion (from the U.S. dollar to the British pound or the Japanese yen, for example). This is what the forex is all about.

Once I found out that I could join in on this market I was very excited. When I dug deep and saw that it was and continues to be the most volatile and most liquid trading market in the world, I was even more elated. Here's the reason: Let's say you buy some big Fortune 100 company's stock, such as Intel, on the NASDAQ. When their quarterly earnings come out, it's good (or bad), and the stock goes up (or down) by 1 percent that month. If you traded the stock properly and placed yourself on the right side of the table, you might have made 1 percent that month. Not very exciting, is it? Now let's look at the forex. Let's say you've been watching the U.S. dollar and you notice that it's strong. The news says that the U.S. dollar is going up against the Canadian dollar, for example. If you watch the forex all day, you'll actually see up-and-down cycles that are dramatic enough for you to make 1–10 percent on your money in one day or even double your money in a week. Why? Because Canadian banks might be working hard to push the CAD up while trading is going on, but pressure that day forces it back down, and the cycle continues.

This is the most important feature of the forex, and I cannot stress it enough: each currency pair—the U.S. dollar vs. the Canadian dollar, the U.S. dollar vs. the Japanese yen, the U.S. dollar vs. the British pound, or the U.S. dollar vs. the euro—will go through ups and downs all day and night almost every day of the year. Within one day or a week, you will see an up-and-down cycle that takes a stock market a month, a quarter, and even a year to go through. Within this daily volatility on the forex, you can make hundreds or even thousands of dollars with very little initial investment of your own (starting with as little as a $500 account).

Think of it this way: if there were pure stability—say the U.S. dollar and the Canadian dollar were on par all day long, one for one—there would be no room for speculation, no room to bet or hedge on one or the other to go up or down. Someone else is thinking that it's going up, you're betting that it's going down, and each of you makes nothing. However, the good news is that there is pure instability on the forex. Yet within this instability there are cycles, some of which are nearly automatically predictable, and in this book you'll learn some methods of predicting these cycles.

This is only the beginning, and it's a great first step for your entry into this market. But wait, there's more! With a computer and an Internet connection, you'll have free trading software—the MetaTrader platform—that is incredibly powerful. It shows you the trends you need to make smart decisions. More importantly, it's an open platform, and lots of programmers have written robots and indicators—software automation using complex math formulas and predictive modeling—to do the trading for you or to predict when you should make the trade. I don't suggest that you purchase a robot and believe the hype that you'll make millions while you sleep, but you *will* make money while you sleep. What you need to do is find the right tools, including these robots and indicators, so that you can set up a trading account that is nearly hands off.

If you do it right, you will lightly touch your account and your robot settings, watch your indicators when you have time, and make sure you take profits automatically when possible and nearly automatically when you sense a trend that is beyond the capabilities of the robot. By proactively managing the right tools, with a little learning curve and patience you will ultimately succeed. Like me, you might start out making $20 per day and then take more risk to start making $200 per day and then grow your profits until making a few thousand dollars a day becomes easy.

Before you get started, I have to tell you that nothing this good comes this easily. Yes, I am a successful American entrepreneur, but nothing has ever come easily to me. Everything I've earned has come from very hard work. I've made and lost millions. On forex, I'm finally trading profitably, because I'm not gambling. I'm patiently managing a system that is nearly always automatically working in my favor. Some would call this scalping or hedging, and there are rules to govern this behavior on the forex. You have to make sure that the way you trade is done ethically and professionally and you don't get flagged as a "scalper," even though most of the forex brokers who try to "manage" the system for you would scalp their mother and father without a second thought.

But hold on; you will learn how to professionally trade and make money daily without being called a scalper. No one was there to give me their winning insights and secrets on how this potentially lucrative market works to our favor, so I learned the hard way, losing much sleep and money until I finally figured it out. I now know how to maneuver through this financial sea of sharks and make enough on forex to finally relax and take time off to write this book for your benefit.

It has been my lifelong dream to help others, so your purchase of my book is a fulfilling and rewarding experience for me. For that I humbly thank you!

Read every page of this book. Then reread them. Do it before you start trading. I'm delivering my results to you in this book, and I hope you'll take advantage of them for your own financial freedom! If you want to sign up for some live training over the Web or contact me directly, please visit my Web site (www.secretforexreport.com).

The accompanying snapshot shows what doubling a $1,000 investment looks like, every month for only twelve months, potentially turning it into over $2 million.

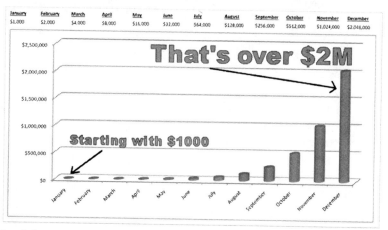

January	February	March	April	May	June	July	August	September	October	November	December
$1,000	$2,000	$4,000	$8,000	$16,000	$32,000	$64,000	$128,000	$256,000	$512,000	$1,024,000	$2,048,000

That's over $2M

Starting with $1000

I wish you much success in your first step to potentially lucrative trading on the forex.

Sincerely,

Sig Samuels

"Nothing gives one person so much advantage over another as to remain always cool and unruffled under all circumstances."

-*Thomas Jefferson*

Chapter One: Introduction to the Forex

The Foreign Exchange Market (Forex)

The foreign exchange market, also called the currency, forex, or FX market, is where high-volume currency trading takes place. It is where banks and other financial institutions facilitate the buying and selling of foreign currencies. Forex transactions involve one party buying a quantity of one or more currencies in exchange for buying other currencies.

The forex market was started in the early 1970s when governments all over the world gradually switched to a floating exchange rate. The purpose of the forex market is to facilitate trade and investment through international currency exchange speculation.

The need for a foreign exchange market came about because of the presence of internationally accepted currencies such as the U.S. dollar (USD), the Great Britain pound (GBP), the euro (EUR), the Japanese yen (JPY), etc., and the need for trading in such currencies.

Today the forex is one of the largest and most liquid financial markets in the world and includes trading between large banks, central banks, currency speculators, corporations, governments, and other institutions.

The average daily volume in the global foreign exchange and related markets is continuously growing. Traditional daily turnover is in the trillions, making it a larger daily market than the U.S. stock market.

Who Participates in the Forex?

The forex is divided into levels of access. At the top is the interbank market, which is made up of the largest investment banks in the world. They control the market and therefore have very close spreads that are not known to the rest of us.

As we get further out of the inner circle, we start to see the difference in bid and ask prices, usually ranging from one to five pips for you and me, the day trader, at the very bottom of the food chain.

International, National, Corporate and Central Banks

A single bank may trade billions of dollars each day on the forex. In general, the interbank market caters to commercial traders, such as multinational companies who have to make payroll in other countries using foreign currencies, and the significantly large amounts of speculative trading every day. Many of these banks will do some of their trading for these large corporate customers, but most of the trading is done using proprietary software behind closed doors and trading platforms for the benefit of the bank.

National central banks play an important role in the forex. They try to control the money supply, inflation, and interest rates and often have official or unofficial target rates for their currencies. They can use their often substantial foreign exchange reserves to stabilize the market, and unlike many banks, they never seem to go bankrupt. Central banks are powerful players in the forex, whether they are winning or losing in their trade strategies and currency-stabilization approaches.

Corporations

A significant part of forex trading comes from the financial activities of corporations that use foreign currency exchange to pay for goods and services. Corporations often trade small amounts compared to banks. As a result, the forex trading of corporations might have a smaller short-term impact on market rates, but their trade flow definitely impacts the long-term direction of currencies. There are some multinational companies that can have an unpredictable impact when they cover very large positions, which might be related to payroll or product manufacturing.

Hedge Funds

Most forex transactions are speculative. This means that the person or institution that is buying or selling the currencies actually has no plans to take delivery or exchange the currency pair. These folks, like you and I, are speculating on the movement of one or more currency pairs (that is, EUR vs. USD, USD vs. CAD, GBP vs. USD, etc.). Hedge funds have been taking a more and more active role in currency trading as part of their overall investment strategy over the past fifteen years. They control billions of dollars in equity, so they can borrow billions of dollars more and can actually move currencies in their own favor by sheer volume and control of their orders.

Investment-management Firms

Investment-management organizations are typically managing large accounts on behalf of customers, such as pension funds, and use the forex to facilitate transactions in foreign stocks. They might purchase and sell several currency pairs to make equity portfolio investments. Some of these firms also use the forex as a pure play on hedging risk for their limited partners by generating profits from the forex. These firms usually have enough assets under management to be able to generate very significant currency pair trades.

Retail Forex Brokers

There are two types of retail forex brokers that provide the opportunity for speculative trading: the retail forex brokers who of course claim that they are working for you and me but in reality might be scamming us while providing an apparent unbiased trading service; and the other group, no longer hidden behind the big green curtain, the market makers. We make up a fraction of this multitrillion-dollar market, while they make up a larger portion of the market. In the United States, forex brokers are regulated by the U.S. Commodity and Futures Commission (see http://www.cftc.gov/) and the National Futures Association (see http://www.nfa.futures.org/).

As I've experienced personally, as have so many others, many retail brokers and market makers are known to trade against us, their clients, and they frequently take the other side of our trades. This absolutely creates a conflict of interest, and many traders like myself want to see them all put in jail. There is a new trend toward what is called no-dealing desk (NDD) and straight-through processing (STP) that is starting to restore retail trader confidence, but caution is advised—trust no one!!!

If you choose to open an account with a retail broker, just make sure you take every precaution I recommend, including keeping an eye on every transaction, reviewing your trading logs frequently for any issues or errors (I cover this in more detail later), and taking out whatever profits you earn as quickly as possible.

Others

Foreign exchange companies that offer currency exchanges and international payments to corporations and consumers use the forex but are not providing speculative trading services; they are actually exchanging hard currencies for a fee. You'll bump into some of these friendly traders at the airport. If you see USDCAD at 1.30, you'll be sure to get a 1.15 or less exchange rate from them, plus they'll hit you up with a transaction fee. You'd be better off going to your local bank where you have an account. The largest provider of this currency exchange service is well known—it's Western Union.

Warning

Before you open any account through a forex broker, you must read this book. Most forex brokers will trade against you and cheat you out of your earnings. They are not all regulated and many use their own very smart robots (trading software) to work your account against you.

Before you take any risk, before you buy any forex automated trading software, known as a forex robot EA (expert advisor), you must read this book.

I guarantee that you will lose money trying to figure out each forex robot and get frustrated with the settings. Then maybe you'll see another robot that sounds too good to be true, buy it, and experience the same disappointing financial loss!

Most forex robots are scams.

Many brokers are scam artists.

Just look at this Wikipedia article from the search term "Forex Scam":

> A forex (or foreign exchange) scam is any trading scheme used to defraud individual traders by convincing them that they can expect to gain a high profit by trading in the foreign exchange market. Currency trading "has become the fraud

du jour" as of early 2008, according to Michael Dunn of the U.S. Commodity Futures Trading Commission. But "the market has long been plagued by swindlers preying on the gullible," according to the *New York Times*. "The average individual foreign-exchange-trading victim loses about $15,000, according to CFTC records," according to *The Wall Street Journal*. The North American Securities Administrators Association says that "off-exchange forex trading by retail investors is at best extremely risky, and at worst, outright fraud."

> "In a typical case, investors may be promised tens of thousands of dollars in profits in just a few weeks or months, with an initial investment of only $5,000. Often, the investor's money is never actually placed in the market through a legitimate dealer, but simply diverted—stolen—for the personal benefit of the con artists."

"In August, 2008 the CFTC set up a special task force to deal with growing foreign exchange fraud."

The forex market is a zero-sum game, meaning that whatever one trader gains, another loses, except that brokerage commissions and other transaction costs are subtracted from the results of all traders, technically making forex a "negative-sum" game.

These scams might include churning of customer accounts for the purpose of generating commissions, selling software that is supposed to guide the customer to large profits, improperly managed "managed accounts," false advertising, Ponzi schemes, and outright fraud. It also refers to any retail forex broker who indicates that trading foreign exchange is a low-risk, high-profit investment.

The U.S. Commodity Futures Trading Commission (CFTC), which loosely regulates the foreign exchange market in the United States, has noted an increase in the amount of unscrupulous activity in the non-bank foreign exchange industry.

An official of the National Futures Association was quoted as saying, "Retail forex trading has increased dramatically over the past few years. Unfortunately, the amount of forex fraud has also increased dramatically ..." Between 2001 and 2006 the U.S. Commodity Futures Trading Commission has prosecuted more than 80 cases involving the defrauding of more than 23,000 customers who lost $350 million. From 2001 to 2007, about 26,000 people lost $460 million in forex frauds. CNN quoted Godfried De Vidts, President of the Financial Markets Association, a European body, as saying, "Banks have a duty to protect their customers and they should make sure customers understand what they are doing. Now if people go online, on non-bank portals, how is this control being done?"

Source: Wikipedia.org

However, there is an exciting, daily opportunity to make a lot of money because of the volatility and liquidity on forex, and there is an equal opportunity to lose a lot of money. I hope that by reading this book, you will avoid the costly lesson that I have experienced in the forex and make it a profitable experience for yourself.

In this book, you will learn how to avoid many of the scams that are out there. You'll also learn the best times to trade manually with intelligent risk management so you can potentially make more profitable trades.

"In this business if you're good, you're right six times out of ten. You're never going to be right nine times out of ten."

-Peter Lynch

Chapter Two: The Forex Basics

What is a PIP?

A pip is the smallest increment in any currency pair. In EURUSD, a movement from .9122 to .9123 is one pip, so a pip is .0001. In USDJPY, a movement from 120.25 to 120.26 is one pip, so a pip is .01.

Typically, when you trade, if you see a currency you are trading move in your direction by ten pips, then you most likely could be making $10. With most brokers, this is of course after you have automatically given them a one-to-five-pip spread—that is, $1–5—just to make your trade.

Your profit or loss in pips is also tied to the lot size you trade and how much margin leverage your broker provides you. You should *never* trade in lot sizes that are too high in risk for your deposit. I'll tell you more about lot sizes later on in this book.

Paying Smaller Broker Commissions

If you live in the United States and you trade USDJPY, the pip spread that the broker automatically takes from you will most likely be smaller than if you were trading EURJPY, for example, because there is a built-in exchange fee that makes the pip spread a bit higher.

So look for USDCAD, EURUSD, USDJPY, etc., where at least one of the currencies in the pair you are trading includes the USD.

The Importance of Fundamental Trading

Fundamental trading strategies consist of a high-level, bird's-eye-view assessment of where a currency should be trading based on just about any criteria except price. The variables you would use to make a decision on where you expect the currency to go (up or down) usually would include the economic conditions of the country that the currency represents, its central banking and monetary policy, and other fundamental elements. This method alone is very difficult to use when dealing with marginable trades and pip spreads, because it does not help you by providing specific entry and exit points. Thus it is very risky to use this method by itself.

There are important economic indicators to watch for while trading on the forex because they will sometimes have an impact on your trades if you are not prepared and when you least expect it.

Some of these indicators of fundamental analysis include the following:

1) Commodity Research Bureau's index (CRB index)
2) The Gross National Product (GNP) deflator
3) The Gross Domestic Product (GDP) deflator
4) Consumer Price Index (CPI)
5) Producer Price Index (PPI)
6) Purchasing Managers' Index (PMI)
7) Durable Goods
8) Employment Cost Index (ECI)
9) *Journal of Commercial* industrial price index (JoC index)

You should run your favorite Internet search engine and use key words like GNP or GDP or CPI and do some research. It's important to know when major reports are coming out, such as the nonfarm payroll report, for example. Be prepared for increases in the volatility of trading during the hours just before and after this kind of news.

The Importance of Technical Analysis

Technical analysis differs from fundamental analysis in that it is applied only to the price activity of the market, ignoring fundamental factors. It can be done on time lines and provide you with a case history of what happened with a currency in the past so that you can attempt to catch a "wave" in the present or the near future.

This method has become the primary one used successfully by day traders who look for short-term price movements on a few currency pairs at a time. To minimize their risk they will set a stop loss and take profit target. Just remember that you can't trust your broker—ever! So when using this methodology, you need to be prepared to surprise them by setting a higher take profit than they expect and a much lower stop loss than you might have wanted and then move these values in by manually recalculating them while you are working on a short-term trade.

The more active changes you make to an order, using a modify order command or feature of your trading software, the more you will confuse untrustworthy brokers and their nasty robots that want you to lose your money.

In fact, you might have to manually close out your good, profitable trades when you reach your take profit goal, because the forex broker's server (running their own robot EA against you) will miss your take profit accidentally but not your stop loss. You have to keep a keen eye on your trades due to the fact that most brokers want you to lose your money.

Most commonly used in the forex, this methodology can help you make successful trades, but do not expect every trade to make money. Sometimes, and especially with forex EAs, you will see three out of four trades go south— yes, I mean in the wrong direction.

I'll cover more on robots later, but technical analysis is very powerful and can work to your advantage in the forex if you have patience and follow common sense, not greed. If you are too greedy, you will lose your money, guaranteed. It's better to use this methodology to "scalp" $100 every morning than to attempt to make $1,000 or $10,000 like many of the false advertising lying robot hucksters will tell you.

Understanding Bars and Candlesticks

There are various types of visuals that traders use to understand currency trends. The best and most basic are bar charts and candlestick charts.

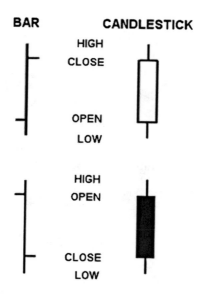

Bar charts display information in vertical lines, representing price action during a given time frame. You can easily see from the bar on the right the low price for that time frame, the opening price, the closing price, and the high price.

Candlestick charts are similar to bar charts; however, they have filled or hollow candles with wicks and tails.

If the candle is hollow, the price at closing during that time frame was higher than the price at opening. If the candle is filled, the price at closing during that time frame was lower than the price at opening.

A bar chart is displayed below:

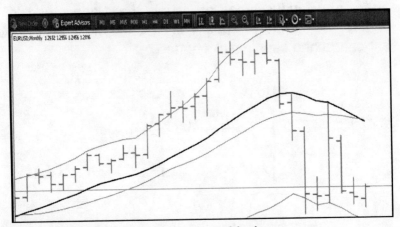

A candlestick charts is displayed below:

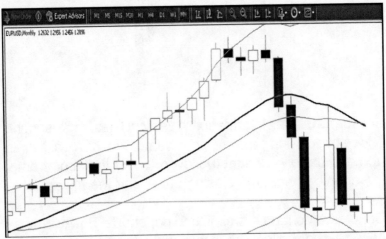

Candlesticks are my favorite. There's a lot of information in a candlestick chart trend. Some patterns you can easily see are shown in the diagram below:

Hammer

You can see a small body near the high with a long lower wick with little or no upper wick. This signifies a bullish pattern during a downtrend.

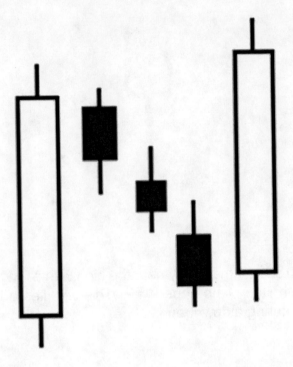

Bullish 3

You can see a long white body followed by three small
bodies, ending in another long white body. The three small
bodies are contained within the first white body. This is a
bullish continuation pattern.

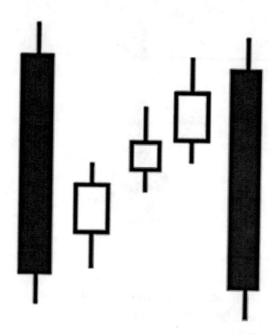

Bearish 3

You can see a long black body followed by three small bodies and ending in another long black body. The small bodies are usually contained within the first black body's range. This is a bearish continuation pattern.

Inverted Hammer

You can see an upside-down hammer with a white or black body. This is a bottom reversal signal with confirmation on the next trading bar.

There are many more patterns to learn about. All you have to do is search for "forex candlestick chart" in your favorite search engine.

Support and Resistance

One use of technical analysis is to derive support and resistance levels. This is easy to understand—the concept is that the market will tend to trade above its support levels and below its resistance levels. If one of these levels is broken, that means the trading direction is moving away from or through the current direction. These levels can be determined by analyzing the currency pair chart that you are currently trading on and looking for past performance to see where the market for this currency has encountered unbroken support or resistance in the past.

For example, if you've never seen the EURUSD go past .9120, then it has a resistance level of .9120. If you see it start to pass this number, chances are it will continue for some time (it could be very short) in the upward direction, so a buy EURUSD trade just as it starts to pass .9120 is a good move, and you should be able to "scalp" some profit (some pips) on this currency pair.

On the other hand, if you see it nearing .9120 and it starts to head south, then a sell EURUSD would be a good trade because historically there is strong resistance at .9120 and it should start to fall. You might place a trade of sell at .9115 with a stop loss of .9125, because it's most likely not going to move above .9120, and a take profit of .9015 so you can pull in ten pips or $10 for yourself.

There is no foolproof way to trade without risk, but there are ways to trade where your profits will be consistently greater than your losses. This is what I'll try to teach you. It's just not possible for all your trades to be positive. The real goal is to manage your risk so you can make more profitable trades than losing trades.

The Premium or Overnight Interest

Every currency has a cost of carry associated with holding onto that position for more than a day. In the forex this cost is a function of the interest rate differential of the two currency pairs that comprise the exchange rate for that particular order.

For example, in USDCAD, the interest rate differential is the difference between short-term U.S. interest rates and short-term Canadian interest rates. If, for example, U.S. interest rates are 3.0 percent and Canadian interest rates are 1.0 percent, the interest rate differential is 2.0 percent (3.0 percent − 1.0 percent).

This means that if a trader was to sell USDCAD, he would have to pay 2.0 percent of the notional amount of the contract per year to hold the position. On one lot, the notional amount is $100,000, so the trader would have to pay approximately $2,000 to hold the position for one year. This translates to approximately $5.40 per day per lot for holding the USDCAD position ($2,000/365).

Warning

Don't start trading real money right away. You will most likely lose it quickly, if you do. As you start to get comfortable with the basic terms, you should still consider opening your first account as a Demo account. It is best to trade on the forex using a demonstration account for the first month or so, while you get a handle on the various aspects of trading. You will learn more about the various methods of trading as well as the bar and candlestick charts by using 'fake' money.

A Demo account with a real Forex broker let's you pick a starting amount of money and trade it on demonstration servers where whether you win or lose, it's not your own money – it's not even real currency. However, you will see all the information you need to see about live currency pair values, the cost in PIPs to make a trade with this broker and other important factors. Don't trust the results of this Demo account to fully match up to live trading, especially using software robots, but assume it will give you the basics you will need when you choose to put real money into a 'live' trading account with this broker.

"Real knowledge is to know the extent of one's ignorance."

-Confucius

Chapter Three: Forex Knowledge is Trading Power

MetaTrader – The Most Popular Software Trading Platform

I don't want to recommend any platform to you in particular, and some brokers offer their own proprietary or custom-built software platforms. However, you'll notice that most offer the MetaTrader platform. It's very popular, so both the few honest and many scam artist robot EA marketers will tell you that their robot is well designed for the MetaTrader platform.

You might get one in thirty robot EAs to work right, and that's good, because then you'll have an automated money-making system. I found some robot EAs and indicators that can work well to help you make a little money every day, but it takes a lot of work to tweak and manage. I will tell you more about this subject later, but you are at your own risk if you try to run a robot on a live account (that is, your money being traded by a piece of software that plugs into the MetaTrader platform).

There are also software indicators available for sale, and you'll get some free indicators with the MetaTrader platform. They will give you signals for market momentum and show you more accurately where the support and resistance lines have historically been on a currency pair graph. Indicators are great for helping you manually trade successfully through technical analysis.

If you don't yet have a brokerage account, you can open one up at one of the major brokers in the forex and they will most likely have their own branded version of the MetaTrader software available for download. If you want to start practicing with this software, you can download a free copy from MetaQuotes Software, the company that makes it on their web site (www.metaquotes.net).

Remember this because it is very important – once you have a live, online trading account, you should un-install the first version from MetaQuotes that you have been playing with and then get ahold of the current downloadable version from your forex broker. Their customized version might be the only version that works with their trading system, so make sure to run only the MetaTrader version they offer.

The accompanying graphic shows what MetaTrader looks like:

When you turn it on by default, it may look a little different. I've set up the platform the way I like to use it, with some key indicators. I'll tell you more about these later when we learn about a method of manual trading that has been profitable for me.

You'll see all your currency pair trading options on the left:

Symbol	Bid	Ask
◈ USDJPY	98.67	98.70
◈ EURUSD	1.2680	1.2682
◈ GBPUSD	1.3758	1.3762
◈ USDCHF	1.1600	1.1603
◈ USDCAD	1.2810	1.2815
◈ AUDUSD	0.6457	0.6462
◈ EURGBP	0.9212	0.9221
◈ EURJPY	125.12	125.16
◈ GBPJPY	135.75	135.84
◈ EURCHF	1.4708	1.4714
◈ USDMXN	15.2413	15.2642
◈ CHFJPY	85.07	85.11
◈ GBPCHF	1.5955	1.5967
◈ EURAUD	1.9628	1.9636
◈ EURCAD	1.6244	1.6253
◈ AUDCAD	0.8273	0.8281
◈ AUDJPY	63.71	63.77
◈ NZDUSD	0.5034	0.5042
◈ AUDNZD	1.2810	1.2827
◈ CADJPY	76.98	77.05
◈ USDTRY	1.7548	1.7579
◈ XAUUSD	895.95	897.00
◈ XAGUSD	12.58	12.67

Market Watch: 23:48:48

Symbols | Tick Chart

Bid/Ask Price Spread

When trading on the forex, all quotes are two-way. There is always a bid and an ask. The ask is always higher than the bid price. The bid price is the price that the dealer is willing to pay to buy the first currency in the currency pair, known as the base currency. As a day trader, this is the price you will get when you sell the currency.

The ask price is the price at which the dealer is willing to sell the base currency. As a day trader, this is the price you will get when you buy the currency. The difference between these two prices is called the spread. The smaller the spread, the better.

Different forex brokers offer different spreads for different currencies, so make sure you are getting the smallest pip spread you can. But don't forget that you want a forex broker who will also cause you the least amount of pain. For example, let's say you pick a forex broker who offers a two pip spread on major currency pairs, so you sign up, move your money into your new account, and then find that they have a slow trading network or use tricks of the trade to hurt you and take your money. Again, be cautious! If their marketing and signup deal looks too good to be true, it most likely is a scam!

Below the currency pairs, you'll also see your expert advisors (robot EAs) and your indicators.

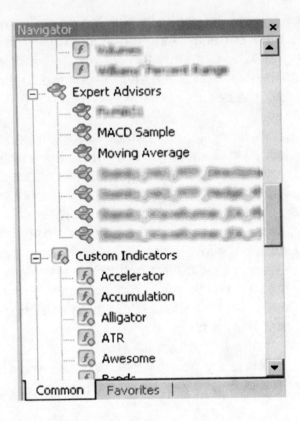

These tools are dragged and dropped onto a currency pairs trading chart, and then you need to properly fill out the settings you want and those that might be required to properly activate these tools.

I've grayed out some of my robot EAs because I'm certain you are not ready to try them. I'll tell you about them later in this guide.

As I said earlier, without proper settings, management, and fine tuning, your own robots could make you go broke very quickly.

On the right, you'll see the current and past trading history on one of the currency pairs you are watching. You can view by minute (M1), five minutes (M5), fifteen minutes (M15), thirty minutes (M30), hourly (H1), daily (D1), weekly (W1), and monthly (MN). It's very important to look at each time line view of a currency, because the trading trends in each time line will give you a bigger-picture view of what is actually happening with the currency pair.

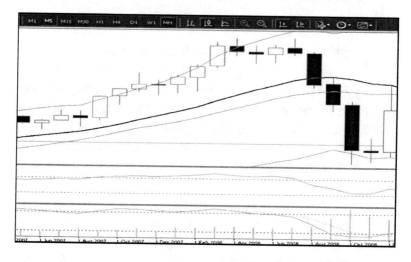

You'll also see your account trading history in detail on the bottom.

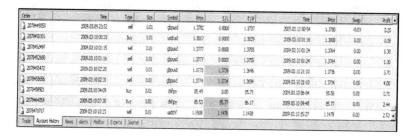

The trading account history window shows you your orders, the time the orders were opened, the type (typically buy or sell), the lot size (notice .01, low risk), the symbol being

29

traded, the price that you put your order in at, the stop loss (S/L) and the take profit (T/P), the time the orders were closed, the price at the close, a swap (for trades that linger overnight), and your profit on each trade.

The Importance of Log Files

LOG FILES: FIND THEM, REVIEW THEM, AND BACK THEM UP

Imagine that you are about to make a smart trade on a currency pair—say you choose the EURUSD and you feel strongly that it will be heading up by ten pips. You set up to make the trade, you watch the currency, and right when it reaches the ten pips of profit, something strange happens. Here is a real example that the forex broker cheats will do to you: they might pop up a message box saying, "Are you sure you want to close out this trade?"

While you are in shock reading this message, the currency pair moves in the other direction by twenty pips, and when you click okay, you lose money! This happens. Your log file will be useful evidence.

You can then call the forex broker support line (after you back up your logs) and make a formal complaint and then ask for your money back or to unwind this trade.

They have their own server logs that show that their own nasty robot caused a pop-up message and this delay in your trade, and if you push hard enough, you can force them to apologize for the "server error" and get the trade undone. They will do many other things to try to steal from you, so watching and backing up your log files is very important. If you installed MetaTrader in the default folder on your C drive, you would find your logs here:

C:\MetaTrader 4\logs.

Copy this entire folder to a backup somewhere at least once a week. To do this you need to create a folder—it can be called anything like "C:\BACKUP"—and then copy everything from the logs folder to your backup folder. The log files will be in text format so you can open them and review them in notepad. Just click on a log and you might see a file like this:

This log looks normal. But if you see text such as "couldn't connect to server" or any other message that looks like an error message, it may be due to the forex broker running a nasty robot against you that could delay orders, not accept orders, force pop-up message confirmation boxes, change the spread without your knowledge in advance, etc.

What They Don't Want You To Know

If you look at all the marketed forex systems out there, most will suggest but not guarantee that you'll see "thousands of dollars in profit each day" or "turn $1,000 into $20,000 in just days." They have very attractive Web sites that make you feel like you're going to succeed if you could just give them your e-mail address, join their system, and then give them your money. Some will issue a refund if you are unhappy, but many will delay paying you back; most folks will just give up asking for the refund.

If you think it's too good to be true, you are right! They might even show you guaranteed back-testing results on a demo account or even a live account.

1) First, back-testing is useless. Never believe back-testing results.

2) Second, they may or may not show you the lot size they used in their supposed trades of past history.

3) Third, most of these results are based on demo accounts, which means that they were run on demo servers that might not have all the nasty broker robots trading against you and other nasty things that will do harm to you. So demo results are the results in a "perfect world" that just does not exist.

If you buy into their service or their system or their robot, you will find that in live results you will most

32

likely be margined out, losing your money very quickly, because the "solution" of choice has way too large a lot size, putting you at incredible risk.

If there is one thing you should remember from my advice, it's this: Never trade large lots. Let me say it again: never trade large lots. *Never.*

If you have $1,000, you should trade no more than ten currency pairs at .01 lot size, setting your RISK at only 10 percent. If you want to trade one currency pair, you should trade no more than .1 lot size at a time. If you have $10,000 to risk, then you could risk trading 1.0 lot size at a time. Just check the screen-printed results closely and you'll see that their demo account was magically able to trade numerous trades at 1.0 to 10.0 lot sizes and they were never margined out. This is absolutely impossible.

Margin: The Most Important Item in Forex

Forex trading is always conducted on margin. This means that your cash deposit into your potentially untrustworthy broker... account is usually much smaller than the underlying value of the currency pair contract that is required to allow you to make the trade. The good news is that you get powerful leverage; the bad news is that you can lose your shirt very quickly. Don't worry; you can't lose more than you put into your account. But margin means multiple and leverage, so you can get bigger trade swings going too quickly where you might see quick large profits and also quick large losses, in which case your friendly broker will automatically close out your margin—that is, you lose all open trades if the overall margin is too far negative, even if you might have had a positive swing in two minutes or two hours. And you won't have time to get money moved to your account fast enough to cover the margin, because their automated system will do its job and sweep your account dry.

This might even happen while you are sleeping. In fact, if you don't properly set a reasonable stop loss, you can expect major losses from overnight trades.

Here's an example: Let's say your friendly broker requires only $1,000 of your cash in an account in your name to start trading 100:1. That means that you can trade $100,000 in currency pair positions. This is powerful leverage. So you start trading in various lot sizes. Now you are in trouble. Here's why.

Lot Size: The Second Most Important Item in Forex

You should *never* trade in lot sizes that are too high in risk for your deposit. For example, let's say you deposit $1,000 and get a 100:1 margin account, and when you start trading currency pairs you decide you want to do a full 1.0 lot on USDCAD and a full 1.0 lot on EURUSD. And you do the same with two other currency pairs. You have four open trades, each a full 1.0 lot size. You see a couple of currencies move in the right direction and you instantly notice $100 of potential profit.

Meanwhile, one currency pair moves south by $1,100. What happens next? The broker freezes your trades, closes your orders, and steals your money, and there's nothing you can do. Oh, they will tell you that you agreed to take the risk and that they stole nothing. Maybe they are right. If it were your stock broker he might be polite enough to call you up and say, "I have a margin call. Do you want to cover it so I don't have to close out the trade?" No, that will not happen on the forex, and you will see your account hit zero in ten minutes or less with a too highly leveraged margin. So what can you do? *Never* trade with more than 10 percent of your cash balance in risk. What does that mean? If you have $1,000, then don't trade more than a total .1 lot size—notice the decimal place. This is the second most important thing you should remember in the forex, or you will learn the hard way!

If you wish to trade four or let's say five currency pairs, then you should divide .1 by five and have a .02 lot size on each trade. If you want to trade ten currency pairs, then set the lot size to .01; that is, take .1 and divide it by ten. Now the most risk you will see might be a $100 to $200 drawdown on your margin but never eating up your cash. If you ever see your margin reach 30–50 percent of your cash, it's time to start taking your losses before you lose everything. That would mean—painfully—yes, closing out some losing trades and getting the margin drawdown to a reasonable number.

Please also note that the margin they will make available to you will be based on your account equity, not your cash balance. That means that they will increase the margin allowed to you if you have open trades that are positive but not yet closed. They will also automatically lower this number if most of your open trades are negative and outweigh the positive, so be careful.

Just remember one thing: if you have $10,000 you can afford one single trade at 1.0 lot size, and that's a 10 percent risk. If you have $1,000 you can afford one single trade at .1 lot size, and that's also a 10 percent risk. *Never* go over 10 percent risk with your open trades and margin. If you do, you had better keep a very close eye on your trade and not sleep at night, because that's when it will keep going south on you, when you least expect it. Then you will wake up very sorry because the friendly broker will have automatically closed you out if your margin is too high compared with your equity. When it's a zero balance on the scale, you will be sorry, so please keep the risk level at 10 percent or less and you'll enjoy your forex experience.

Warning

Although brokers in the United States are supposed to be regulated by the U.S. Commodity and Futures Commission (see http://www.cftc.gov/) and the National Futures Association (see http://www.nfa.futures.org/), many U.S.–based brokers will say they haven't yet been "accredited" or they are working on it and have filed their papers. You should check with the CFTC if you have any questions about brokers in the United States. If you are in another country, check with your local government. Try to do an Internet search on the broker and see what kind of feedback they have received. Just use the broker's name and the word "scam" and then dig into the search results and see what you find. Remember what I shared with you from Wikipedia.org on "Forex Scams" and be very cautious.

Beware of paid advertisement search results, because many of these will lead you to true scam-artist products and services.

Even many forex blogs and apparent forex product reviews are not trustworthy. They are just trying to hook you with fake stories, and if you buy some crappy forex EA product or sign up with a crappy forex broker by following a link off their site, you'll find that these are really advertisement links to their commission, Yes, these "independent reviewers" get paid to recommend forex robots, so don't trust them.

Trust your instinct—does it seem like a well-marketed site? Are they telling you that they "reviewed all the scams and found these good ones"? Most likely the "good ones" are really bad, and they get paid as affiliate advertisers to send you over to the bogus brokers, products, and/or services.

"Success is going from failure to failure without loss of enthusiasm."

-Winston Churchill

Chapter Four: Opening Your Forex Account

Finding the Right Broker

Never trust your forex broker. They are there to be profitable, greedy and take you for everything you have. If they have excellent customer-support phone service, it's because they want you to open an account and start trading (most likely losing money to them).

I could give you a list of forex brokers, but then you might blame me for pointing you in the wrong direction. Just do a search on the Internet using your favorite search engine for the keywords "forex broker" and do your own research to find one.

Remember to also search for as much feedback on them as you can find and then contact them; visit them if you can, find out how solid they are, ask them who they do business with in retail banking, and check up on them at their local, well-regulated bank.

Find out who their CEO is and get every piece of data you can before you sign up with them so you know who to go to later when you catch them cheating you.

Remember, finding the right broker is not that easy, because most of them should be locked up! My upcoming book might be entitled *"Winning a Lawsuit Against Forex Broker <INSERT NAME HERE>.* Have I said it clearly enough? *Don't trust them!*

Remember, many will promise to take "small" pips in their commissions, but they won't tell you that they are trading against you at the same time. So you might close a trade early due to losses in their favor, or worst case for you, you might watch the market go in a direction you did not expect while they sit on the profits.

You can still make money with these criminals if you are smart about managing your margin risk and lot sizes and take your earnings out as quickly as possible. If you understand what they will do to you before you take the risk, you can avoid the many pitfalls they will place in front of you. If you get greedy and move your lot sizes up and maximize the margin, you will lose everything. It's really up to you to take my advice and be very cautious when trading forex. Don't get greedy, avoid the pitfalls, and cash out quickly at least 50 percent of your positive earnings every month as long as they are not eating into your margin.

Where to Open an Account

If I haven't scared you off, then try to open an account with a forex broker who is physically located in the same country as you are. Even better, find one who is close enough for you to pay them a personal visit (one—to check them out; two—to be able to visit them on site and demand your money if it ever came to this).

What Is a Forex ECN broker?

ECN stands for electronic communications network. A forex ECN broker does not have a dealing desk but instead provides you with an opportunity to join multiple market makers, banks, and traders to directly enter competing bids and offers into the platform and have your trades filled by multiple liquidity providers in an anonymous trading environment.

The trades are done in the name of your forex ECN broker, thereby providing you with complete anonymity. A trader might have their buy order filled by liquidity provider "A" and close the same order against liquidity provider "B" or have their trade matched internally by the bid or offer of another trader. The best bid and offer is displayed to the trader along with the market depth, which is the combined volume available at each price. A greater number of marketplace participants providing pricing to the forex ECN broker leads to tighter spreads. ECNs typically charge a small fee for matching trades between their clients and liquidity providers.

The chances of your orders being "accidentally" screwed up by a forex ECN broker are much slimmer than the problem happening with a standard forex broker. Also, if you have enough capital, you can become your own forex broker and cut out one risky layer, but that discussion is for another day. Visit http://www.secretforexreport.com/ecn to learn more and for a list of forex ECN brokers that I have been able to find. I can't guarantee any of them, so please do your due diligence and check them out first.

Getting the Most Tax Benefits

If you are really serious about becoming a forex trader, you should start to think about this as a business. This means you might want to create an "S" corporation or an LLP or LLC. For example, if your name is John Smith, you might want to incorporate "John Smith Forex Trading LLC" in Delaware or your local state.

Then, every expense you have related to trading on the forex could be leveraged as a tax write-off—your home office, your computer, your car, gasoline/miles you travel for forex training (even visiting your local library), etc.

I recommend that you talk with a tax professional such as your family accountant or any friends you have who understand how to do this. There will be some start-up expenses and annual filings you'll have to do, but the benefits, if you are really serious about the forex, will far outweigh the risks of not doing so.

Warning

I've had an account with a well-rated, supposedly reputable forex broker, one of the largest in the industry. When I asked for some of my money, they kept losing the wire transfer paperwork. It took me three weeks to get the money that they promised I'd have within three to five business days and "usually three days for wires." No matter which broker you choose, you need to stay on top of them and make sure that when you want your profit, they aren't floating it for their own benefit for too long. By the way, they will take your money to open an account within minutes or hours, but getting your earnings out is another story.

So make sure you get all the information regarding how to get your money out right before you open the account. Talk to someone in customer service, get their name and extension, and ask them if they will guarantee that when you fill out the necessary form and fax it in you'll see your money as promised. Ask them for the name and telephone extension of the individual who runs the outbound wire transfer department. Tell them that you won't open your account until you have this information, and see how they react.

"Where large sums of money are concerned, it is advisable to trust nobody."

-Agatha Christie

Chapter Five: Working with Robots

What is a Forex Robot?

There are two types of forex robots – those that automatically trade currency pairs on your behalf and those that provide you with automatic indications and alerts as recommendations for your manual trading strategy.

Auto-trading Robots

Trading automatically on the forex is achieved by installing an additional piece of software known as an auto-trading forex robot into the proper folder on your hard drive, where you've installed your MetaTrader platform. Once you drag and drop a robot onto a currency pair chart and enable the software, buy and sell orders will automatically be placed by the forex robot.

Forex Indicator Robots

Forex indicator robots are installed into your MetaTrader platform the same way as an auto-trader robot, however, they are placed into the indicators folder. Once activated, these robots do not automatically trade. However, they will provide you with powerful indications such as when to buy or sell a currency pair.

Avoiding Robot Scams

There are so many forex robot expert advisors (EAs) on the market, it's really hard to tell which ones actually work. Some are forex robot indicators, which tell you when they think you should buy or sell a currency. Today, all robots do technical analysis only and are unable to do fundamental analysis.

However, one would hope that with the advent of the RSS (really simple syndication), one day robot EAs will "subscribe" to an RSS news feed on a particular currency and other related market news and be able to parse this information to help the robot decide whether or not it truly is a good time to buy or sell a currency. For now, though, this is just a pipe dream, so expect your robot EA to only be able to look at past or current time line trends to attempt to best determine the direction a currency will be headed.

Some robots are fake; in other words, they are designed to work properly with your trading platform but there is no intelligence in their decision making. When you find this out one or two months after spending $50 to $500 on the robot, it may be too late to get your money back.

Most of the folks selling these robots assume that some percentage of their customers will not ask for a refund or make getting a refund very difficult.

Some robots are indicators, and others are actual expert advisors who will trade live for you automatically with your demo account or live account.

If it's an indicator, it will most likely tell you to buy or sell, but you'll have to make the choice and manually execute the order. If it's a true robot EA, it will do the work for you. Some robots can set stop loss and take profit settings on a currency order, and others cannot. Really smart robots can deal with the nasty "counter" robots running at the forex broker and misrepresent a stop loss or take profit number to your benefit by setting an initial stop loss and/ or take profit that's far away from reality. Then, as your order nears the profit mark, the robot EA will modify the order and move these numbers in your favor when it's too late for a broker to mess with your order; and you'll make your money.

There are blogs and Web site reviews of robots, and it's also hard to tell which ones you can trust. Visit my site (http://www.secretforexreport.com/robots) for a list of all the robots I've tried and some ideas on what to watch out for (such as no stop loss, lot sizes too large) and what kind of settings you'll want to see in any robot that you're willing to risk your money on.

I also have a page about indicators that are good for manual trading because you still get to make the final decision on an order (http://www.secretforexreport.com/ indicators). I do *not* recommend trying any of them without doing intense research.

Finding Robots That Work

If you do an Internet search on "forex robot" or "forex robot EA," you will find many advertisements and links to various robots, with most links telling you how great each robot is at making money for you. You might get hooked on a robot because of the fancy marketing, big-dollar winning claims, and at least two or three video testimonials. Be cautious!

So far, I have only found a few forex robot EAs and indicators that work. However, the caveat is that they cannot just run and make you money without some level of risk. For example, Steinitz HAS MTF actually does what the inventor, Don Steinitz, claims: "100 percent no loss system" and "enters profitable trades automatically."

Here's the catch: If the robot is making you $20 per day on a $5,000 account, within a month you'll see a drawdown of as high as $2,000. That means that while you are earning money with positive closed trades, others may stay open for a long time until they turn profitable and the robot can close the order. Because this robot does not use take profit or stop loss until the very end of the trade cycle, when it can close the trade profitably, you will see a growing margin risk if you don't manage it properly. So is it truly a 100 percent no loss system? Yes, if you have enough time and money to risk while it keeps closing smaller positive trades.

Tuning Robot Settings

It's important to know the GMT offset for your broker and to ensure that your robot allows you to set it correctly. Here are some sample broker offsets:

- Alpari: GMT +2
- CFGTrader: GMT +2
- CoesFX: GMT +3
- Fibo Group: GMT +2
- Forex LTD: GMT +2
- FXCM: GMT –4
- FXDD: GMT +3
- IBFX: GMT
- Marketiva: GMT
- MetaQuotes: GMT +2
- MoneyTec: GMT +3
- Netdania Charts: GMT –8
- North Finance: GMT +2
- Oanda: GMT –5
- Orion: GMT +4
- Real Trade: GMT +2

GMT offset also varies with daylight savings. For example, a GMT + 2 is from fall to spring, and GMT + 3 is from spring to fall. These numbers might also change if the forex broker moves their server from one time zone to another, so it's best to confirm the GMT offset with your forex broker when you open your account.

Why You Need to Own a Root Server

If you are going to risk running a forex robot, you absolutely *cannot* run it on a home computer or even a highly recommended virtual private server. Do not fall for either of these apparently low-cost ways to start a forex robot trading for you.

Here's why:

1. If you lose Internet connectivity, most forex robots will not be able to properly close out their trades. However, if they set a static (never-changing) stop loss and take profit, then you should be okay.

2. If your personal computer needs a reboot due to an upgrade or a patch or if you lose power, your forex robot will crash. This means that when you reload the MetaTrader or similar trading platform, you'll have to restart your forex robots and they will not remember anything about their prior trades.

3. A virtual private server (VPS) will most likely be rebooted every Tuesday after a patch upgrade from Microsoft® or if/when the provider feels like it. That means that all the work you do to set up your forex robots will have to be redone when you log into your VPS only to find that it was recently rebooted without your knowledge, consent, or permission. And you'll have no say in the matter.

If you are trading with forex robots, it's worth the investment of $100 per month, about double the cost of a VPS, to get yourself a root server running Microsoft Windows® Server that supports the MetaTrader or similar platform, not running in sixty-four-bit mode. You'll want it to be running in thirty-two-bit mode so your trading platform and forex robots will work. If, by default, it's not running in this mode, you can ask for it to be re-imaged to a Windows® environment in thirty-two-bit mode. This only takes the hosting company about an hour.

Once you have a root server running, you should install only two other pieces of software other than your trading platform and forex robots. One is a free tool called Shutdown Guard, and the other should be your favorite anti-virus software; a good one you can get free is called Comodo. This should keep your root server free of viruses and keep it from rebooting. Also make sure you turn off automatic updates under the Windows® Control Panel. For more information, please visit my Web site (http://www.secretforexreport.com/rootservers).

Forex Peace Army: A Free Up to Date Resource on Robots

I strongly recommend you join the Forex Peace Army (www.forexpeacearmy.com) as it is by far one of the very best free resources on the forex. When looking into robots, you want to avoid being scammed. The Forex Peace Army offers free, live reviews. On their web site, you can read reviews left by other traders and you can also watch the results of robots trading on Demo accounts.

In addition, the Forex Peace Army has a database with over 17,000 searchable forex reviews. I strongly recommend you go to their web site and sign-up immediately. Then, click on the performance tests menu item and click on equity weekly to sort the list of robots under evaluation. Check out the robots that appear to bring the most PIPs weekly and then look at the live Demo account trades. Make sure you take notice of the opening balance – is it $500.00 or $50,000.00? Then, look at the lot size of the trades – is it a full 1.0 lot or a .01 lot? These are important factors. You'll also notice the most popular or successful currency pair trades of each robot. If it a currency pair that does not include your local currency, such as the USD or CAD in the United States or Canada, for example, then you should also expect these trades to have a higher cost per trade in PIPs, taken by your dealer, if you do not trade directly through an electronic currency network (ECN).

Visit the Forex Peace Army frequently, join the forums, post questions, read the questions and answers posted by others and most importantly, learn about the robots without having to do it yourself and then ask for your money back because it doesn't perform to your expectations, or worst case, you find out your robot is a piece of scam software.

Warning

If robots worked as advertised, I'd be retired by now! Only a few of these forex robot vendors appears to be for real, but the catch is that *no* robot will make money for you without you being very smart about when and how you use it. If you just simply turn it on and let it manage your money, assume that you will lose all of your money within a few days, weeks, or a month at best.

"We simply attempt to be fearful when others are greedy and to be greedy only when others are fearful."

-Warren Buffett

Chapter Six: How to Trade Manually

Basic Manual Trading

Now that you have the basics, I'll share with you how I trade manually for profit. First, I use four basic steps for all of my trading:

1. Preparation
2. Pricing
3. Entry
4. Exit

Preparation: After you have studied the market conditions, read the news on your currency pair (I recommend starting with only one pair—try EURUSD first as it has consistent cycles that are more predictable than others), and logged into your MetaTrader or similar platform, you'll set up your key indicators: ADX, moving averages, and Bollinger Bands.

If your trading style is for large pip swings, expect this to take a significant amount of time— maybe a few days or a week. This requires you do more detailed analysis of longer-term trends including fundamental analysis and to carefully manage your drawdown risk as you will not be watching your trade while you are sleeping. If you want to trade on smaller, quicker time frames with less pip profit and risk, you'll be scalping and will need to do so during the most volatile hours I've suggested earlier, such as between 7:00 AM and 9:00 AM EST. If so, it's very important to focus on short-term chart analysis. I strongly recommend that you review multiple indicators to confirm your decision.

Then, when you see a clear pattern—some trend that appears consistent—you've checked the support and resistance levels and you see an opportunity to set up a trade to buy or sell a currency pair. You're now ready to begin the next step.

Pricing: Here you have determined that there is a trend moving upward or downward and you've seen a trend over various time frames (typically you should check M5, M15, M30, H1, D1, and W1), although sometimes these trends will not match; for example, when a short-term trend shows a currency pair falling, but in the bigger picture, say for the day or week, it's actually working its way upward.

Now you have to decide whether you are day-trading or forex scalping. If you are day-trading then you'll see a price trend over a period of an hour, a day, or a week that helps you choose your stop loss price and your take profit price. If you are forex scalping, make sure you are doing this in the specific morning or evening hours I've suggested earlier and be prepared to make very quick decisions. You'll leave enough room on stop loss and take profit to make money or reduce the risk of losing too much. Then you are ready to move on to the next step.

Visualizing Currency Pairs for Trade Entry

There is a really powerful free indicator I found that's available at my site (http://www.secretforexreport.com/indicators) called the relative strength basket-trading system.

This powerful indicator lets you look at all major currency pairs with upward green arrows and downward red arrows on each time frame, all on one screen. Credit is due to Kang Gun for writing such an amazing MetaTrader platform-visualization tool.

Here's how it can help you be sure it's time to enter a trade: If you choose to trade, for example, EUR vs. USD or EUR vs. CAD, you'll notice from the chart above that the better choice would be a sell EURCAD because the CAD has been on a strong upward trend while the EUR has been on a strong downward trend.

You can see positive and negative numbers on the total upward or downward pip swings of each currency with numeric values and then the darker arrows showing the strong trend in the time frame and the lighter arrows showing a weaker trend in the time frame. This is a really powerful tool that you should learn to use as an additional visual indicator to help you confirm when it's time to enter a trade.

Entry: In this phase, timing and price are very important, because you are initiating a trade with the least risk of loss according to your own analysis. Here's where you will create an order with your forex broker, setting a stop loss and a take profit that leave you room for the currency swings that happen throughout the trade cycle. For forex scalping, it's best to enter only one trade at a time, or at most a few good trades. Why? Because you will be getting out quickly and you will want to manually move your stop loss and take profit numbers as the currency swings. Can you watch more than two screens at a time? Most people cannot, unless they have multiple monitors and drink way too much coffee.

Once you are in a trade, you automatically will lose money with a forex broker if you try to jump out immediately, so the timing of entry is important. This is because instead of charging commissions at the end of a trade, they have a pip spread where you will need to see the currency move in your direction at least two or more pips before this trade can break even.

So now that you have entered a trade, if it's a longer day-trade cycle, you should not have to watch it until the next phase of the cycle. If you think a currency is going up over a daily period (D1), then you should really expect to see your results the next day. Watching it every five minutes does not make sense and only causes stress.

If you are scalping, then you'll be watching the currency pair for seconds, minutes, and possibly, but most likely not, hours. Why? Because you intend to catch a wave of currency pair direction as the wave begins and then when you reach your take profit, just before the wave ends, if possible.

Watching your trade in various time frames using the following indicators will help you reduce risk: RSI, stochastic oscillator, ADX, moving average, and Bollinger Bands.

Exit: In this phase, if you are scalping, you should plan to exit your trade as quickly as possible, profitably. It's better to make five pips than to lose fifty. Continuing to use the suggested indicators, you should see the currency pair move closer to one of your two exit points, either the stop loss, which is initially a risk-reducing loss, or your take profit goal. Once you see that your trade is beginning to show a profit, it's a good time to modify your order and set the stop loss to actually be a profitable number, some number of pips below your current profit depending upon the volatility of the currency pair at this time. If the pair is making quick multiple or large pip swings, this won't work because you'll hit the new stop loss number and have your trade closed with a very small profit. The real goal here is to keep moving your stop loss closer to your profit goal: this is called a trailing stop loss. But what if the currency pair never reaches your take profit goal? It could be stuck below the resistance line or turn around on you and head in the other direction, hitting your stop loss later on. So it's also a good idea to manually close an order that is above a profitable stop loss and close enough to your original take profit goal.

If you are not scalping, then make sure you take a close look at each currency pair as they each have different characteristics. For example, EURUSD has a consistent sine wave–like motion, while GBPJPY is extremely volatile and may move in large unexpected swings. Use technical analysis to reaffirm your take profit goals and to review the daily currency pair news. If you set up the trade properly it will usually close within a day or two and will automatically exit when it reaches your take profit or stop loss.

Leveraging Market Calendars and Indicators

Before opening any new trades, you must understand what is happening in the two currency pair markets you are about to trade. For example, if you are going to trade the great British pound (GBP) versus the U.S. dollar (USD), are there any major events that can impact your forex trading which are scheduled for this day, week or month? For these two currency pairs you would look up information that can affect each currency.

For the GBP, you will need to find out the calendar for these variables and if any being updated today, this week or this month it will affect your trade: PPI output, Bank of England interest rate decision, Bank of England asset purchase target, BRC retail sales, manufacturing production, trade balance non EU and total trade balance. For the U.S. dollar, you will want to see if the private Federal Reserve Bank or the U.S. Treasury is coming out with any major announcements such as in increase or decrease in interest rates. In addition, the U.S. dollar has a calendar of announcements such as consumer credit, short-term diesel output, short-term natural gas output, automotive production, mortgage applications, job loss claims, retail sales and the big one – non-farm payroll.

I've created a web page with hyperlinks to all the major world currency calendars to keep your eyes on at my web site (www.secretforexreport.com/calendars).

Best Times to Trade

The best times to trade are dependent on numerous factors, the most important being the following:

1) Are you calm and in the right frame of mind?
2) Can you clearly read important news that might affect your trades?
3) Are you willing to watch the currency pair charts patiently?

If you don't feel well or have too many interruptions, don't trade. Wait until you have a clear head and peace of mind. If you are nervous or distracted, you will most likely make a mistake and risk losing money on each trade you do right now.

Okay, so now you are ready to trade, right? Well, there are other factors that are important for making trade decisions:

1) Fundamental news (nonfarm payroll report, GDP update, etc.): Make sure to get the forex news the night before and then right before you start trading in the morning. Spend fifteen minutes reading the news on those currency pairs that you are considering making trades on that day.

2) Multiple time frame technical analysis of a currency pair: You need to look at the M5, M30, and H1 at a minimum if you are forex scalping. If you are day-trading, you'll need to do the same, but also look at the D1 and the W1 time frames. Remember that these are five minutes, thirty minutes, hourly, daily, and weekly time frames.

Day-trading is about opening a currency pair position and setting a stop loss and a take profit such that you can leave the trade alone and assume that either it will hit the stop loss or the take profit automatically while you do other tasks (your day job, sleep, etc.).

By reading the news and comparing the time frames you might see a pattern such as the euro grows strong against the USD today (or this week) or the USD strengthens against the CAD or the JPY weakens with today's news. When you see JPY vs. USD dropping, then you can confirm that the news has been helpful, and if you are planning on selling the JPY vs. the USD today, you might pick up some profit based on the news and the D1 (daily) candlestick chart trend.

Forex scalping is about opening and closing a currency pair position in seconds or minutes. Even though scalping involves the use of leverage from your available margin, the trades can be higher risk. However, the short period of time you are in a trade decreases your risk exposure, because you won't be holding a position for very long.

If you can do this right, you'll make a reasonable amount of money every morning or every evening that you can trade. The best days to scalp are Monday through Thursday from 7:00 AM–9:00 AM EST and 7:00 PM–9:00 PM EST plus Friday mornings from 7:00 AM–9:00 AM.

During these times, there is an incredible amount of volatility among the following currency pairs:

EUR/JPY—Euro/Japanese yen

EUR/USD—Euro/U.S. dollar

EUR/CHF—Euro/Swiss franc

GBP/USD—British pound/U.S. dollar

USD/JPY—U.S. dollar/Japanese yen

USD/CHF—U.S. dollar/Swiss franc

USD/CAD—U.S. dollar/Canadian dollar

AUD/USD—Australian dollar/U.S. dollar

You might notice other currency pairs moving drastically up and down for these two hours each week morning and evening except Friday evening, when the market is closed.

Find a currency pair you like and watch it for a half hour for drastic changes, either downward swings, upward swings, or a constant up-and-down zigzag. Here's where there is money to be made. If you see a currency pair moving upward, you'll just want to track key variables to make your decision that it's a good buy or that it's a good time to short it, a good sell.

The data you need comes from various market indicators. Those I use include the following:

1. ADX

2. Moving average

3. Bollinger Bands

By using indicators and reviewing them across different time frames, you will see trends. Gaining an insight on a currency pair trend is the way to make intelligent day-trading or scalping decisions.

I'll explain each of the tools I use. To add them to your MetaTrader currency pair, just open your indicators list and then simply drag and drop these indicators onto the chart. You might want to read the documentation and set a few properties, or simply go with the defaults.

Use ADX (average directional index) to gauge the intensity of a trend's strength. The ADX is a classic measure of the strength of a trend. Unlike Bollinger Bands and moving averages, which can help define the direction of the trend, the ADX simply measures whether the trend is strong or weak. The index is displayed as an oscillator in a separate box below the price charts on a scale of zero to one hundred. As a rule of thumb, if the ADX is greater than thirty, a trend is strong; if the ADX is below twenty, a trend is weak. In a strong trend, we want to see the ADX sloping upward.

Moving averages track the average price of a currency pair over a specified period of time and are one of my favorite tools for identifying a trend in the currency market. By definition, moving averages track the average price of a currency pair over a specified period of time.

A ten-day simple moving average (SMA), for example, tracks the average price of a currency pair over the past ten days. A good way to identify trends with moving averages is to look for a perfect order. This occurs when all of the shorter-term moving averages are above the longer-term moving averages in an upward trend and the longer-term moving averages are above the shorter-term moving averages in a downward trend. You will usually see a new and powerful trend emerge when these perfect orders form after a period of range trading.

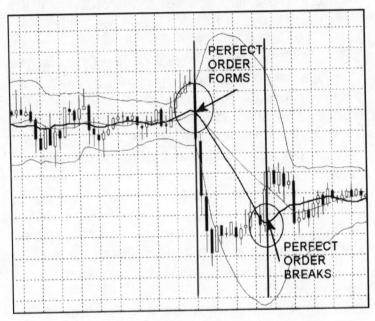

Bollinger Bands forecast when a currency pair may enter or exit a trend. They basically plot standard deviations above and below a moving average. They were developed in the early 1980s by John Bollinger and are typically used to determine volatility. I like to use them to gauge a trend.

You can get a feel for when to buy and when to sell. For example, when an upward trend in a currency pair is very strong, it will remain in the buy zone, the zone between the upper Bollinger Band of two standard deviations and the upper Bollinger Band of one standard deviation, for some time.

When the downward trend is very strong, the currency pair will remain within the sell zone, the zone between the lower Bollinger Band of two standard deviations and the lower Bollinger Band of one standard deviation. If the currency pair closes below the buy zone or above the sell zone, we say that it has entered the range-trading zone.

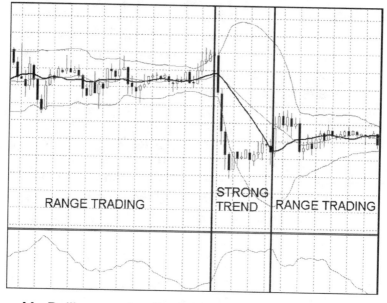

RANGE TRADING   STRONG TREND   RANGE TRADING

Mr. Bollinger notes the following characteristics of Bollinger Bands:

1. Sharp price changes tend to occur after the bands tighten as volatility lessens. Traders call this "the squeeze," and it's a good time to watch for either a rapid upward trend or a rapid downward trend depending upon where the candles are headed.

2. When prices move outside the bands, a continuation of the current trend is implied. So when you see the candles moving out of a band, that's the direction you should consider trading.

3. Bottoms and tops made outside the bands followed by bottoms and tops made inside the bands call for reversals in the trend. This is the good old "what goes up, must come down" adage, and the reverse also usually holds true. A move that originates at one band tends to go all the way to the other band. This is a sine wave–like pattern that you should look for so you can enter near the top or bottom of the next sine wave for potential maximized profits.

These Bollinger Bands are great tools to use to help determine when a currency pair enters or exits a trend. If you like to begin trading by picking a top or bottom, a good way to do so is to wait for the currency pair to exit the buy or sell zones.

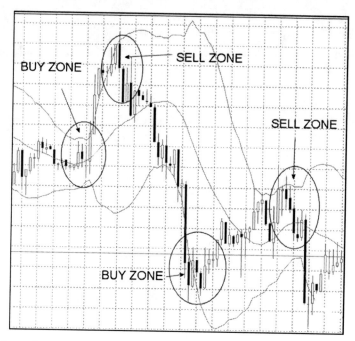

Warning

Don't expect all of your trades to close positively. Your mission is to manage and control risk, stay calm, track the market trends using technical and fundamental indicators so that the majority of your trades close positively. Remember that six out of ten trades closing positively can mean the difference between losing money and gaining profits. If you expect to close nine out of ten or all trades positively, you're not thinking clearly and your goals are unrealistic. Use the basics in preparation, pricing, entry and exit and you should do fine.

"Insanity is doing the same thing over and over again and expecting different results."

-Albert Einstein

Chapter Seven: Advanced Manual Trading Methods

Now that you have learned manual trading, it's time to discover some powerful methods of advanced manual trading for increased daily profit potential. Although there are hundreds of methods, many books and e-books on the subject, I've picked the three that are the most fundamental and powerful methods you can learn quickly. Remember, no method is perfect and not all trades are winning or profitable. These methods are highly successful if used correctly. Remember to make sure you study the current market trends. As the forex is so volatile, you cannot predict an outcome that will be correct all the time, but you should be able to increase the odds of successful trades by intelligently using these advanced trading methods.

Fibonacci Method

Leonardo da Pisa who is also known as Leonardo Fibonacci was an Italian mathematician, considered by many to be the most talented of his time (c. 1170 – c. 1250). He is most famous for developing the numerical sequence that is widely known as the Fibonacci numbers or sequence.

The first number in this sequence is zero and the second is one. The sequence then develops as each subsequent number is the sum total of the previous two numbers, known in mathematics as a recurrence relation. You're probably wondering what does this have to do with forex trading?

Well, as Leonardo Fibonacci discovered that this Fibonacci sequence and their ratios could be found everywhere throughout the natural world, existing almost as universal rule. These numbers are important for charting and as a powerful forex indicator.

In fact, there are books on how to use his method for the U.S. Stock Market and the forex. One of the better places to learn more about this method is the Forex Fibonacci web site (www.forexfibonacci.com).

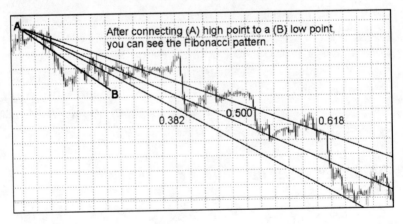

The three most important Fibonacci numbers you need to remember are 0.618, 0.500 and 0.382 or 61.8%, 50% and 38.2% respectively. There are other important Fibonacci numbers, but for starters these are the ones to use. You will use these numbers to calculate retracement levels which will help you decide when to place a buy or sell order on a currency pair. If a currency pair is trending upward, then history tells us that at some point this currency pair is going to hit a peak and go into at least a temporary decline or reversal, and then resume the upward trend. When it starts the reversal, that's where the Fibonacci numbers come into play. You can visualize this Fibonacci sequence by drawing what looks like a seashell with an inner circle growing into an outer circle or smaller and then larger circles as seen below:

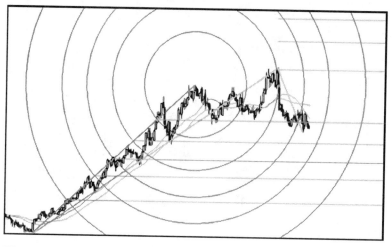

The price of the currency pair that you notice to be following an upward trend is usually predicted to reverse or decline backwards to one of the key Fibonacci numbers, and then bounce back again to follow the upward trend. The key is to forecast this point accurately so that you can buy-in before the trend continues upward, so that you can capitalize on the reversal and then profit. There is a free Fibonacci indicator that ships with MetaTrader and you can of course, purchase more complex Fibonacci indicators from commercial sources. Once these levels are identified, horizontal lines are drawn and used to identify possible support and resistance levels. Your goal will be to enter a trade as close to a Fibonacci retracement as possible. If you get in at the first retracement, when a currency pair is trending upward, your order will be for a sell, to jump in on the temporary decline or reversal. You will then close out that trade and initiate a buy order when the currency pair resumes the upward trend.

Correlation Trading

One of the best advanced methods is called correlation trading. In fundamental trading methodologies most folks look at one currency pair at a time. For example, you've been watching the U.S. dollar vs. the euro, and you've followed my recommended four steps in trading: preparation, pricing, entry, and exit. You've been noticing that the current trend might be that the U.S. dollar (USD) is dropping in strength against the euro (EUR). If this is true, then why, on the same type of time frame chart, would you notice the U.S. dollar (USD) increasing in strength against the British pound (GBP)? It should be obvious that a normal trend would be the EUR and GBP both going *up* against the USD at the same time if the USD is weakening against one of these currencies.

Let me give you some other correlation-trading examples. If the price of a barrel of oil is going up, shouldn't the price of air travel go up as well? So if you are watching oil and you also watch airfares, you should see them go up together or down together. Here's another example: if the price of rubber trees has been dropping dramatically, shouldn't the price of tires go down as well?

So these are two separate trades to watch for, but they should be in sync. When the GBPUSD currency pair is rising on the one-hour chart (H1), shouldn't the EURUSD currency pair also be rising on the one-hour chart (H1) at the same time? On most occasions, the answer is yes.

Why is this so exciting? Because no matter your style of trading, whether you are quickly scalping pips or swing trading or long-term trading, all of these trading styles can take advantage of correlation. By watching GBPUSD and EURUSD currency pairs on the H1, H4, or D1, for example, in any of these matching time frames these separate currency pair charts should be correlated! If the USD is going up against the EUR, then it should also be going up against the GBP. If the USD is going down against the EUR, then it should also be going down against the GBP. It's that simple.

Here are some sample charts that prove this fundamental analysis:

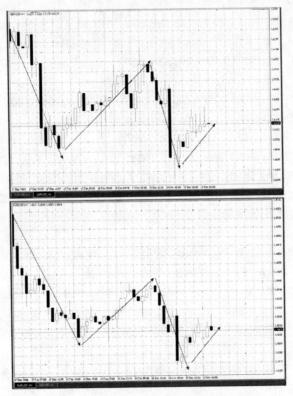

While these separate currency pairs, EURUSD and GBPUSD, are in sync, you should trade as you normally would. In this case, it's an opportunity to buy both currency pairs against the USD. If you want to make an advanced correlation trade, from the H1 graphs above, now is not the time. However, while watching these two currency pair charts, if you notice that the trends do not match, then you have a correlation-trade opportunity. As we can see below, an opportunity for a correlation trend has opened itself up, and we could make hundreds of pips by trading both currency pairs during this time. For this short period they are out of sync with the actual current strength of the USD, and this is a great opportunity to make a trade.

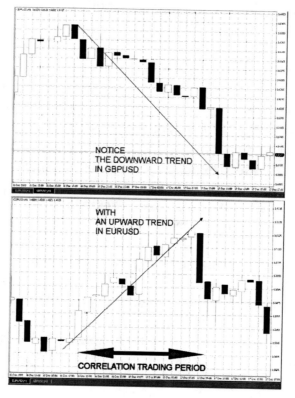

NOTICE
THE DOWNWARD TREND
IN GBPUSD

WITH
AN UPWARD TREND
IN EURUSD

CORRELATION TRADING PERIOD

What you need to know as this trend begins happening is where the initial setup happens, when it triggers a buy or sell decision, how to minimize our risk with stop loss, and when to exit the trade for our take profit.

The entry point for a correlation trade is when you start to notice a break in the trends moving in the same direction. Trading correlated pairs using two charts at a time may seem like a slightly more complicated way to trade, but the key to successful trading is having straightforward signals. There could not be a better set of signals as to when these two charts get out of sync. The results can allow you to take profit regardless of whether you are scalping or day-trading. It really doesn't matter which method you choose as long as you properly manage your risk.

Trend Surfing

After looking at the correlation-trading method, let's explore one more unique way to trade money. I'm not sure if I invented it, but I've definitely come up with a name for it—I call it trend surfing. In this style of trading, we're going to consider world events, which is a fundamental analysis. It is apparent that some of the elite power bankers have decided to push the USD down over the long haul. I believe that this is a current trend.

This means that over the next year we should see the USD continue to drop, while gold, a "hard" currency, continues to go through the roof, breaching the $1,000 USD per ounce barrier. The euro is also a favorite currency of this elite group—folks who can trade a billion USD in a day and not even break a sweat. So I would look at the EUR vs. the USD as a strong "soft" currency vs. a "weak and soft" currency.

Does this mean you should jump into this trend and start trading EURUSD with as much as you can afford? Yes and no. Yes, because the trend appears to be real and will happen for a long period, at least a year, but no, because if you don't know how to properly surf this trend, you will be margined out along the way.

Trend surfing is to "ride the wave" that some powerful market leaders have decided to create—yet you will ride this wave in a way that keeps you on their wave and not drowning along the way. To do so, you need to ensure that your account has enough margin so that this long-term trade opportunity is a wave you can afford to ride. Here's why: What these market makers will do while they are pushing the USD down is to fake out other traders daily. Yes, right when you've joined this wave, you expect it to just ride up and up and up, but in reality it goes up and down in the short haul while the very long-term trend shows that it is going up.

So there will be folks who join the wave and put in a full 1.0 lot order on an account with only $2,000. And what will happen? They will appear to be making money on the EURUSD order for a few hours and then wham! The EUR drops against the USD quick enough and deep enough for a 1.0 lot to risk your entire $2,000 balance, and you get margined out. These elite are sweeping you clean.

The only way to make it on their wave is to surf their trend—it's moving onward and upward, but along the way they will purposely make large trades against the current trend, making the wave dip down quickly and deeply, just long enough to cause "the little guy" (that's us) to be foolishly margined out.

How can we trend surf? Let's say we have a $2,000 balance in our forex account. The only way we can surf this twelve-month trend of the USD going down and down is to only trade a fraction of our account such that we can leave the trade open even if the wave dips down against it for a short period.

If you trade .01 lot size EURUSD, even if it dips down deeply, the drop in pips will not be low enough to margin you out, so day after day, this single trade will ultimately be growing. And after one year, this tiny trade might turn into something much bigger.

Take a look at the following picture to visualize what I mean by trend surfing:

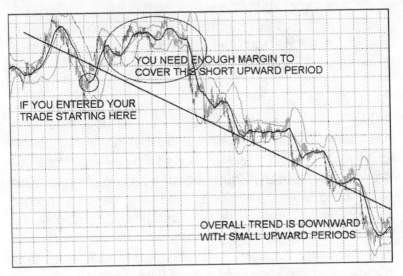

YOU NEED ENOUGH MARGIN TO COVER THIS SHORT UPWARD PERIOD

IF YOU ENTERED YOUR TRADE STARTING HERE

OVERALL TREND IS DOWNWARD WITH SMALL UPWARD PERIODS

So now you've learned another important way to take advantage of what some of the market makers have decided to do. If you hear more and more news about another currency being weakened, you can assume that one of the elite favorite currencies is going to get stronger and stronger.

This will always create a trend-surfing opportunity, where you can put a small and reasonable trade on autopilot during this trend as long as you control the size of your trade and all other open trades such that your risk of being margined out is as small as possible.

Warning

Advanced manual trading can be very challenging and very risky. You must fully comprehend the method you have decided to use for each trade. If you are uncertain as to the mechanics of the method, then you have increased, not reduced, your risk. Make sure to do additional research on the methods described herein and try them on a Demo account first. Don't be impatient – if it takes you a month or two to learn an advanced trading method and for you to gain confidence, that's ok. With patience, your chance to profit is much greater.

"Only those who risk going too far can possibly find out how far they can go."

-T.S. Eliot

Chapter Eight: Managing Your Risk

A Balanced Approach

It's no secret that you need to manage your risk. If you expect to make a profitable, winning trade every time, you are wrong. Simply put, if you trade intelligently, you will do your best to have more profitable trades than losing trades. As I've recommended repeatedly, do not risk more than 10 percent of your account balance as the cumulative total of all your open trades. The real trading model that works is to focus on small profitable trades that provide the least amount of risk. Do trades that are between 1 and 10 percent of risk of your account balance only one at a time.

If you want to manage more than one trade, keep the total risk of trade A + B less than or equal to 10 percent of your account balance. If you trade a full lot (1.0 lot) on a $10,000 account balance, you are at risk, easily, of up to 10 percent of your account balance. I've seen one full lot go negative by $1,000, and yes, I've seen it go positive by this amount as well in a matter of hours during very active trading times. Imagine that you leave a few trades open at 1.0 lot size and go on vacation. When you come back, you might be down $2,000, or 20 percent of your investment. I doubt you'll come back from vacation and see it go positive by this amount. Why? Because you aren't managing your risk.

Using Stop Loss

The way to do this is to watch your trades and create a minimal level of risk through a stop loss. You can set a stop loss on a trade that you are certain is moving in the right direction so that if it does go south you only lose a little of your hard-earned investment on this one trade. You can also set a take profit so that while you are away, if it reaches a reasonable, not greedy, profit margin, you'll (usually) automatically have that order close positively. Remember that all brokers are greedier experts than you and know how to manage their risk; if they can fool you or your robot they will make you miss your take profit number. To manage this risky situation, it's best to set stop loss instead of take profit as a moving, sliding number moving upward in the direction of your trade. That way, when your trade makes you ten pips, you might set the stop loss at two pips, so you are guaranteed to make a profit if the trade direction turns. Then, if you see it hit twenty pips in profit, you could move the stop loss manually to twelve pips profit, and so on. You pick the risk factor that you are comfortable with, but the real secret is to keep wringing out the risk by moving your stop loss closer and closer to your take profit target.

If you cannot manage your risk, expect losses. This is the root cause of loss. Did I say that loud enough? *The root cause of loss is no risk management.* You should look for profits *after* you manage risk. The winning forex traders manage risk first—they assume that they will lose on every trade. They plan to get out of each trade with the least losses. This is the opposite of how you would normally think. Most folks think "making profits" and "winning" is exciting, so you focus on this first and risk last. Big mistake! If you have to kill a trade because it's not a winner, you have to get out and move on to the next opportunity. Managing risk does sound boring, but it's actually the most exciting and important thing you can do.

Watch Your Open Trades

You'll also need to keep a keen eye on your open trades. I actually do not like to have more than one or two trades open at a time. It might seem like you are missing out on more exciting market opportunities, but the reality is that it's very hard to manage more than one or two trades at a time. If you end up opening up too many trades, you'll be frantic to watch them, especially moving from one currency pair to another.

So to manage your risk, only have one or two open orders per day. If an order is stuck open for longer than you expect and you see an opportunity to open another trade, just remember that you are now increasing your drawdown. This could also put you above the 10 percent number I've repeatedly recommended. Don't be greedy; learn to be patient. It's better to make $100 over two or three days than to have a negative $300 in open trades that are heading south.

Take Profit Sliding Window

Remember how important it is to ensure that every order you place has a stop loss and a take profit set to a range you can afford. If you make the stop loss too many pips away, you might see a deep drawdown. If you make the stop loss too few pips away from the current price at your order entry, you might see a quick closeout of the order because of a short-term dip or spike in the currency pair.

One good way to manage your risk is to manually modify orders that are starting to show profit by locking in your profit. You can modify orders and move the stop loss above the original entry price if the current price is far enough above that point, heading toward your original take profit number so that you lock in your profit. However, as I've seen some hiccups with forex dealers' servers, you might want to manually close the order if it has reached your take profit range. You might win or lose a few pips, but you'll know that your order was closed profitably.

Getting Your Profit Fast

Find out from your forex dealer how quickly they will return to you any of your cash investment and profit. Ask them *before* you open an account how long for a wire transfer, how long for a paper or electronic check, and what forms (get copies of these in advance) you will need to fill out to get your profit into your bank account and back in your hands.

And remember to ask specifically who is currently working in the wire department and call that individual and confirm the time frame that the salesperson promised you. For example, they might say that it takes five days for a check and three days for a wire.

Also find out if there is a fee for checks or wires or both. When you ask for your money, make sure you don't take too much out, leaving any open trades at risk of a stop-off or margin call. If you can take out half of your profits once a week or every two weeks or once per month, you will be in good shape.

Warning

Most forex traders lose their shirts because they think about risk management last, not first. I cannot warn you in any stronger or clearer way – if you do not manage your risk for each and every trade, you will not be successful on the forex. Also, don't be too greedy. If you see a trade that you like and are sure you can close it positively, what are you waiting for? Why not set a trailing stop loss and a sliding take profit so you can lock in a winning trade? If you trade lot sizes that are too large, or decide to open just a few extra trades without controlling your margin, you might be drawn down too deeply to recover and lose on all of your open trades because you get stopped out. Be smart, focus on risk management first and foremost.

"Good judgment comes from experience; and experience - well, that comes from bad judgment."

-Anonymous

Chapter Nine: What to Do if You've Been Ripped Off

I was hoping not to have to write this chapter. You never know when you've tried everything, followed all my Warnings and yet you still find yourself a victim from a forex scam. The best thing you can do if you've been ripped off is to stay calm and collect as much evidence as you can to prepare your case.

If you've been ripped off by a forex scammer, here are some powerful ways to attempt to reap the rewards of justice. Please note that I am only describing your options in the United States. If you live somewhere else, you may find that in your country, there are similar reparation and consumer protection programs available to help you if you have a claim for damages against a forex scammer. If the free options I propose don't get you the results you want, it may be time to build your case, hire an attorney and sue the company that scammed you.

CFTC's Reparations Program

The CFTC's Reparations program is designed to provide an inexpensive, expeditious, fair, and impartial forum to handle customer complaints and resolve disputes between futures customers and commodity futures trading professionals. Part 12 of CFTC's regulations, 17 CFR 12, contains rules relating to Reparations. If you are a futures or options customer, or a leverage contract customer, and you have a dispute with your futures trading professional that you cannot resolve, you may be able to use the Reparations program if:

- Your complaint involves a futures trading professional registered with the CFTC at the time of the alleged wrongdoing or at the time you file the complaint.

- You allege that the individual or firm involved—the proposed respondent or respondents—has engaged in activities that violate the Commodity Exchange Act or CFTC rules. The transactions involved can include futures contracts, options on futures contracts, or on physical commodities, and leverage contracts. You must outline facts in your complaint to show that the losses you claim as damages result from the activities you describe and that the proposed respondents you name engaged in these activities.

- You file your complaint within two years of the date the violation occurred or within two years of the date you should have known about the violation—the statute of limitations.

- The proposed respondents you name are not

in bankruptcy or receivership and you are not pursuing the same claim in a parallel proceeding such as arbitration.

- If you are a foreign resident, you must file a non-resident bond.

Be aware that the information provided here is not legal advice. If you think you need legal advice from a private attorney, review CFTC's section on "do you need an attorney" located on their web site located here:

www.cftc.gov/customerprotection/redressandreparations/
reparationsprogram/index.htm

Check Their Registration Status

Complaints must involve a commodity futures trading professional registered with the CFTC who is alleged to have engaged in activities that violate either the Commodity Exchange Act or CFTC regulations. Check registration status of futures trading professionals with the National Futures Association's BASIC or contact the CFTC's Office of Proceedings.

Alleging Violations or Illegal Activities

You must allege one or more violations of illegal activities in your complaint and provide evidence to support your claim. Illegal activities include, but are not limited to:

- **Fraud**: cheating or attempting to cheat you through false claims concerning the likelihood of profit or loss; false or misleading statements about trading or about your salesperson, advisor, or the trading program you use; or false or misleading statements about any other material fact that you relied on in making a decision about futures or option trading.

- **Breach of fiduciary duty**: a failure by a broker or salesperson to act with special care in handling your account when required to do so by the Commodity Exchange Act or CFTC rules.

- **Unauthorized trading**: trades made by a broker without your prior specific authorization or a written grant of authority to effect trades without your specific authorization.

- **Misappropriation**: a broker's unauthorized use or diversion of money that you deposited for the purpose of trading futures or options.

- **Churning:** excessive trading of your account for the purpose of producing commissions and with disregard of your financial interests.

- **Wrongful liquidation**: the unauthorized closing of your position.

- **Failure to supervise**: Failure by a supervisor to diligently oversee the handling of a customer account by the supervisor's partners, officers, employees, and agents.

- **Nondisclosure**: failure to inform you of the risks associated with futures and option trading, and the failure to disclose any other material fact you required to make a decision about futures or option trading.

Additional Criteria for Filing a Complaint

Before your claim can be considered under the CFTC's Reparations program, you must satisfy these criteria:

- **Statute of limitations**: Your complaint must be mailed to the CFTC Office of Proceedings within a two-year period after your cause of action accrues—the date when you knew or should have known of the wrongdoing. The appropriate filing fee must be sent with your complaint.

- **Bankruptcy or receivership**: The proposed respondents are not in bankruptcy or receivership proceedings. If so, your claim will be dismissed as to that proposed respondent, and you will be referred to the bankruptcy trustee or receiver appointed by a court to administer customer claims.

- **Parallel proceedings**: You must not be pursuing a claim based on the same set of facts in arbitration or a civil court.

- **Non-resident bond**: Complaints filed by non-residents of the United States must satisfy additional criteria. See Section 12.13(b)(4) of the reparations rules.

Select The Type of Proceeding

Before filing a complaint, you must choose which of the three types of Reparations proceeding you wish to begin:

- the voluntary proceeding (available for claims of any amount),

- the summary proceeding (for claims of $30,000 and less), or

- the formal proceeding (for claims greater than $30,000).

Filing a Complaint

Complete CFTC Form 30: Reparations Complaint Form. The complaint and the appropriate filing fee may be filed in person or sent by certified or registered mail to the CFTC's Office of Proceedings. The Reparations Complaint Checklist is a convenient tool to use to confirm that you have included all necessary information with your complaint.

A complete complaint must include:

- **Information about you**: your full name, address, telephone and Fax numbers, and those of all other persons lodging the complaint (the complainants).

- **Information about respondents**: the names, addresses, and telephone numbers (if known) of all individuals and firms against whom you are filing the complaint (the respondents).

- **Facts**: a statement of facts which supports your claim that there has been an alleged violation and attaches all documents which support or explain your claim, such as account forms and trading statements.

- **Liability explanation**: an explanation of why each respondent you have named should be held liable (any respondent whose liability or involvement is not described may be dismissed from the case).

- **Damage calculation**: the amount of damages claimed and a brief explanation of how you calculated them. The amount you claim cannot be adjusted after the case is forwarded for adjudication except by permission of the presiding judge. Review how to calculate damages.

- **Parallel proceedings statement**: a statement that no arbitration or civil court litigation is pending based upon the same facts and including the same respondents you have named.

- **Bankruptcy or receivership statement**: a statement indicating whether to your knowledge any of the respondents are involved in bankruptcy or receivership proceedings.

- **Verification**: a statement that the facts set forth in the complaint are true to the best of your knowledge, belief, and information. The reparations complaint does not have to be notarized if you sign the reparations complaint form or include a verification statement with the description of the complaint. The verification statement should be written as follows:

"I hereby affirm (under penalty of law) that to the best of my knowledge the facts set forth in this complaint are known or believed to be true."

- **Proceeding selection and filing fee**: you must select the type of proceeding and submit the appropriate filing fee at the time you submit your complaint.

- **Filing Fee Payment**: The filing fee check or money order should be made payable to the Commodity Futures Trading Commission (CFTC).

- **Mailing Address**: Please send your reparations complaint and filing fee to Commodity Futures Trading Commission, Office of Proceedings, 1155 21st Street, N.W., Washington, DC 20581.

How to Calculate Damages

If you are filing a complaint, please review the information below for your calculation of damages by type of claim.

- For misrepresentation, fraudulent solicitation, fraudulent omissions, and other types of claims, you are entitled to be put back into the position you would have been in if the violation had not occurred. This figure is usually your net out-of-pocket loss for the transactions affected by the false statements (i.e., the amount deposited minus any amounts returned).

- For churning, you are entitled to a full refund of commissions generated by the broker during the period in which your account was churned.

- For unauthorized trading, you are entitled to the total losses for all unauthorized transactions (this figure is not offset by profitable unauthorized trades because proceeds from profitable trades always belong to the customer).

- For lost profits it is your burden to prove that any lost profits would have been earned if the violations had not occurred. Such claims for lost profits are obviously difficult to prove. You will have to prove exactly how the trading would have occurred and this cannot be based on mere conjecture or hindsight about profits that might have been earned had the violation not occurred. If you intend to claim lost profits, you must provide a calculation of the lost profits; submit supporting documentation that provides the price of the contract and the date that you intended to sell it; and a full explanation of why those profits should be awarded. Price information is available from the Wall Street Journal at their web site (www.wsj.com) or the Investor's Business Daily at their web site (www.investors.com).

- For unauthorized/wrongful liquidation, the measure of damages is determined by either (1) the value of the options positions when liquidation occurred, or (2) its highest intermediate value between notice of the conversion and a reasonable time thereafter during which the positions could have been replaced had that been desired, whichever is higher. The CFTC decision in Ahlstedt v. Capitol Commodity Services, Inc. [1996-1998 Transfer Binder] Comm. Fut. L. Rep. (CCH) ¶27,131 at 45,291 (CFTC) 1997, and citations therein, provides further guidance.

Interest

The Commission amended its regulations to clarify that post-judgment interest shall run on all reparations awards resulting in judgment for the complainant. The losing party is required to pay post-judgment interest on the reparations award (as well as any prejudgment interest ordered by the presiding official). Such interest shall run according to the terms of 28 U.S.C. 1961 and pursuant to 12.4079d) of the reparations rules. The losing party is liable for post-judgment interest even if the post-judgment interest is inadvertently omittted from the decision that imposted the reparations award.

Review of Complaint

The Office of Proceedings will review your complaint to determine if it meets the criteria for a valid claim.

- If your complaint does not meet the criteria, CFTC staff will notify you of the reasons why.

- If your complaint might meet the criteria but is deficient, CFTC staff will notify you of the deficiencies and give you an opportunity to correct them.

CFTC staff will notify you when and if your complaint has been accepted.

When your complaint is accepted, the Office of Proceedings will forward copies of the complaint to the individuals and firms you named as respondents. Respondents may reply to the complaint by either paying you the full amount of damages claimed or a lesser sum mutually agreed upon as full satisfaction of the claim; or by filing an answer denying any liability to you. Respondents are required to send a copy to you (and all complainants).

Note that in certain circumstances a respondent may file a counterclaim with the answer to your complaint.

CFTC staff will review the answer and your case will be assigned to a judge. If no answer is received from the respondents, CFTC staff will forward your complaint to a Judgment Officer who may issue a default judgment.

Withdrawing a Filed Complaint

Before your complaint is forwarded to respondents, you may withdraw it by notifying the CFTC in writing that you wish to withdraw your complaint—a Notice of Withdrawal.

Once you have sent the CFTC a Notice of Withdrawal, you may:

- refile your complaint with the CFTC (with a new filing fee) provided the two-year deadline has not expired; or

- file your claim in another forum if you wish, such as arbitration or in a Federal or state court of law.

Your filing fee will not be refunded.

After your complaint has been forwarded to respondents, you may not withdraw your complaint without the consent of the respondents. When you have obtained that consent, the CFTC will issue an Order of Voluntary Dismissal.

You may not refile your complaint with the CFTC once an Order of Voluntary Dismissal is issued.

Assignment to Judge

Once CFTC staff determines that a reparations proceeding has met the specified requirements, the case is forwarded to the CFTC Proceedings Clerk for assignment to a presiding judge. Voluntary and summary proceedings normally are assigned to a Judgment Officer; formal proceedings are assigned to an Administrative Law Judge. You will receive a notice of the assignment to a judge, which will also authorize you to begin gathering evidence in support of your claim.

Ex Parte Communications

After you are notified that your case has been assigned to a judge, you may not discuss the facts of your case with the judge or any member of the judge's staff without the other parties being present or, in the case of a written communication, without simultaneously sending a copy of your letter to the other parties. This prohibition against ex parte communications applies to all parties to the case. If you violate the rule against ex parte communications, your case may be decided against you.

Evidence: the Discovery Process

You may provide evidence in support of the allegations of your complaint in many forms, including:

- affidavits (i.e., sworn statements) of the parties themselves and of other witnesses;

- solicitation mailings;

- telephone records, including memos of telephone conversations;

- correspondence;

- account forms, including account opening documents, trading statements, order tickets, and confirmations; and

- other records such as tape recordings.

Parties are responsible for gathering their own evidence.

To obtain evidence that is in the hands of the other side or held by third parties, each side may make a formal request during discovery.

- **Requests to parties**: all parties are required to respond to relevant discovery requests.

- **Requests to non-parties**: the judge can issue a subpoena to obtain information from non-parties.

Discovery requests can be in any or all of three forms:

- **Interrogatories**: questions posed to other parties concerning factual matters (such as names of witnesses, the reasons for a trade recommendation, or the dates of a respondent's employment);

- **Requests for production of documents**: documents held by the other side (for example, a request could be filed to produce copies of order tickets or monthly statements); and/or

- **Requests for admissions**: factual matters that are important but not likely to be disputed (for example, a party could request the other side to admit that the account was first opened on a particular day or that a deposit or trade occurred on that day).

No party may request personal tax returns or personal bank records during discovery unless the judge grants permission.

Abuse of the discovery rules can lead to sanctions, including assessment of costs against the abusing party.

Monetary Awards

Payment in 45 days. Under the law, the respondents must pay you any award within 45 days unless one of the respondents appeals the decision.

Failure to pay. If none of the respondents appeals the decision and the respondents do not pay your award, the Commission will automatically revoke the license and trading privileges of any respondent who fails to pay and fails to report to the Commission that payment has been made. The industry and the public is notified of the revocation and suspension through publication of the CFTC's Reparations Sanctions in Effect.

Collection of an award. The Commission cannot help you collect your award. You may obtain a certified copy of your decision from the CFTC's Proceedings Clerk. If the respondent does not pay the award, you can attempt to enforce the award by filing a certified copy of the reparations decision in the U.S. District Court that is in the district where the respondent lives or has a principal place of business. If the District Court enforces the award, the court normally will require the respondent to pay all court costs and any legal fees incurred in enforcing the award.

Interest. The Commission amended its regulations to clarify that post-judgment interest shall run on all reparations awards resulting in judgment for the complainant. The losing party is required to pay post-judgment interest on the reparations award (as well as any prejudgment interest ordered by the presiding official). Such interest shall run according to the terms of 28 U.S.C. 1961 and pursuant to 12.407(d) of the reparations rules. The losing party is liable for post-judgment interest even if the post-judgment interest is inadvertently omitted from the decision that imposted the reparations award.

Counterclaims

Filed by respondent. A respondent can file a counterclaim against you if it stems from the same set of facts that are the subject of your claim. Counterclaims usually seek to recover a debit balance in an account you held with the respondent. If a counterclaim is filed against you, you will be sent a copy and you must file a reply within 30 days.

Decision against you. If a respondent wins a counterclaim against you, you must pay the counterclaim within 45 days after the decision unless you appeal to the Commission.

If you fail to pay the counterclaim and you do not appeal, the respondent can enforce the award in the U.S. District Court in your district. If you win your claim and a respondent wins a counterclaim against you, your award will be reduced by the amount of the counterclaim award or vice versa.

Additional Resources

Federal court decisions involving commodity law and CFTC decisions in both reparations and enforcement cases are available on Lexis-Nexis and Westlaw and are published in the Commodity Futures Law Reporter (published by Commerce Clearing House). These resources are available in many libraries and most law libraries.

If you are representing yourself, you are not required to cite legal cases, but if you can provide the judge with references to similar cases, you may strengthen your claim.

Registration Information and Disciplinary History

Information about CFTC enforcement or reparations actions is available from CFTC staff in the Office of Proceedings. Information about both registration status and disciplinary history for registrants is available from the National Futures Association.

Bankruptcy or Receivership

If the respondents are in bankruptcy or receivership, you should contact the respondents or their lawyers for the names of the bankruptcy trustee or receiver to determine if you may file a claim.

Arbitration and Alternate Dispute Resolution

Information about arbitration to resolve commodity futures disputes is available from

1. National Futures Association on their web site (www.nfa.futures.org).

2. American Arbitration Association on their web site (www.adr.org).

Futures exchanges offer arbitration programs for disputes involving one or more exchange members.

Filing Civil Cases in U.S. District Court

Information is available from the Clerk of any U.S. District Court. Court information is available from libraries or on the Internet.

Do You Need an Attorney?

Many parties represent themselves; in other words, act pro se. You may not need an attorney if:

- the facts and issues are simple and you can present your case satisfactorily without the assistance of an attorney; or

- the amount of money at stake is so small that hiring an attorney would not be cost-effective.

Remember that when you act pro se, you must gather evidence, comply with all rules and deadlines, and make your own legal arguments. Neither the judge nor CFTC staff will litigate or investigate the case on behalf of any party, whether or not that party is acting pro se.

If you have a complex case or anticipate difficulty in following the reparations rules, you may wish to hire an attorney to represent you. You can ask a local bar association for a referral to an attorney.

Other Resources

There are numerous resources available to you, free of charge. You may choose to contact your state or federal Attorney General's consumer protection office. If you believe you've been a victim of inter-state or inter-country crime, you can contact your local U.S. Federal Bureau of Investigation (FBI) office. Visit the FBI online at their web site (www.fbi.gov) and find out who will help you file criminal charges in your local FBI office. Don't forget to post your complaint online at the Forex Peace Army web site and contact the Better Business Bureau as well. If you dig deep, you'll find so many resources available to help you at no charge. If you've truly been a victim of a forex scammer, when you get done with them, they will wish they never scammed you.

Warning

Formalizing a complaint against a forex scammer is a serious matter. You should organize all the information you can in advance of your complaint. Make sure you have your log files or related financial records handy as evidence. If you are certain you've been scammed, it's up to you to take action against the scammer. Don't just rush to judgment or contact the government when you are angry. Take a day or two to breath, think about the situation and start to document it. The least amount of emotion you put into the process of collecting the evidence and preparing your case, the better for your health and reputation. When you contact the government or an attorney, if you are armed with the evidence and information in advance, you'll be more productive and most likely see a successful outcome.

"Your life is your journey and no one else's. There are no excuses only challenges and obstacles to test your will. If it comes to you but once, why not make it your best life ever?"

-S.G. Samuels

Chapter Ten: Conclusion

Don't expect to become an overnight millionaire on the forex. You will need to heed all of my Warnings, take your time, manage your risk and be very patient. In such a volatile and highly leveraged market, you have the opportunity to lose your shirt as much as you can leverage a small starting balance to generate huge returns. If you find an automated trading robot or indicator you like as well as some manual methods that work for you, a year from today, you might be writing the next book on the forex. The opportunity is yours – let your forex journey begin.

Bigger Than The Stock Exchange

As you have now learned, the forex market is much bigger than the U.S. stock market. On average, over three trillion dollars are traded daily, making this a huge market of opportunity to quickly lose your shirt or intelligently increase your net worth more rapidly than you thought possible. Because of the sheer size and leverage power, you will have the opportunity to make profits consistently.

Higher Risk/Reward Ratio

However, with great power, comes great responsibility. You're now about to embark on a financial mission to grow your net worth in a sea of forex sharks, corrupt forex brokers, fraudulent forex robots, and the fact that money is (normally) neither created nor destroyed; it simply changes hands. This means that when you profit on the forex, someone else has to lose. So, now you have the opportunity to gain great rewards with much higher risks than you will find elsewhere. The volatility of the forex market can be used to your advantage if you act responsibly, professionally and manage your risk.

Avoid the Pitfalls

I've attempted to cover all the possible pitfalls you will face on the forex. By now you've read and re-read my Warnings. You should be able to grow your wealth and avoid the pitfalls. If you do get scammed, you'll also know how to deal with this situation.

Make Intelligent Decisions

Ultimately, by being very intelligent about whom you choose to work with as a forex broker and whether you are going to use any forex robots, making sure that there is some degree of predictable functionality that leads to profits, remember that whether you trade manually or by using these robots, you must prepare to lose some trades in return for a majority of emotionless, profitable decisions.

You cannot control market forces, but when you understand them, you will learn how to ride and even predict the next wave to your own profit and freedom. Never be greedy, and take your profits out as quickly and as safely as you can so you can gain the financial freedom and independence that you deserve.

Manage Risk for Profits

As I've recommended repeatedly, do not risk more than ten percent of your account balance as the cumulative total of all your open trades. The real trading model that works is to focus on small profitable trades that provide the least amount of risk. Do trades that are between one and ten percent of risk of your account balance only one at a time.   By setting trailing stop losses and sliding take profits, you should be able to see a majority of your trades closing positively. Keep a close eye on your open trades and watch for market news that could have a dramatic effect on these trades. Close them if you feel they are at risk, even if you make a little profit, break even on these trades or lose a little, while avoiding larger losses. Risk management is all about making emotionless, intelligent decisions. You should plan on six out of ten trades making you profit as a success. Don't expect to see all trades closing positively and don't be too greedy or you will lose your shirt.

Consistency Brings Results

By now, you should feel confident that there is an untapped opportunity for profits in a huge market. You should also be cautious about those who market to you with products and services in this volatile market. It is up to you to focus on and mange your risk while making consistently profitable trades. Remember that knowledge is power so the more information you have and are able to test through Demo trading accounts, the better off you will be at making smart investment decisions on the forex. Having more consistently winning trades over losing trades will be the key to your financial freedom.

Warning

If you feel I've given you too many warnings or feel so scared now that you are afraid to join the forex then this is your final warning – do it. Just do it intelligently and you'll be fine. I've warned you about all the possible pitfalls I could think of so you wouldn't step on any land mines or be eaten alive by forex sharks. With this knowledge, you should be more than ready to take on the forex challenge and attempt to double your money each month, almost automatically. Good luck and much success to you – you've been warned.

Notes

Keep a good set of notes as you move you way forward – from learning the insights to setting up a Demo account to 'live' trading on a real account with real money.

Glossary

A
* Ask Price: The lowest price at which a currency pair will be offered for sale.

B
* Balance: The total financial result of all completed transactions, including deposits and withdrawals on your trading account.

* Bar Chart: A chart where each vertical bar indicates the highest and lowest prices for a period of time, such as a five-minute bar, a fifteen-minute bar, a daily bar, etc. The closing price and opening price are displayed as ticks on the bar.

* Base Currency: The first currency quoted in a currency pair on forex; for example, in USDJPY, the U.S. dollar is the base currency.

* Bear: Belief that prices or the market will decline.

* Bid: The highest price at which a currency pair will be purchased.

* Broker: A trading firm acting as an intermediary to bring together buyers and sellers for a commission or fee.

* Bull: Belief that markets or prices will rise.

C

* Cable: A term used to describe the exchange rate between the U.S. dollar and the British pound. It originally referred to a cable used for the first trans-Atlantic communication.

* Candlestick Charts: Charts identical to a bar chart in the information they convey but presented in a way to describe price movements.

* Carry Trade: An investment position of buying a higher-yielding currency with the capital of a lower-yielding currency to gain an interest rate differential.

* Channel: An upward or downward trend whose boundaries are marked by two straight lines. A break above or below the channel lines signals a potential change in the market trend on this currency pair.

* Commission: A fee charged by a broker or agent who carries out your transactions or orders.

* Contract (unit or lot): The standard trading unit on certain exchanges. A standard lot with most forex brokers is 100,000 units of the base currency, which is $100,000 USD (that's a lot of leverage).

* Cross Currency: A pair of currencies traded in forex that does not include the U.S. dollar.

D

* Daily Charts: Charts that encapsulate the daily price movement for the currency pair traded.

* Day-Trading: The process of entering and closing out trades within the same day or trading session.

E

* Euro: As of January 2002, the legal tender (monetary unit) of the European Monetary Union, used by the twelve countries in the union: Germany, France, Belgium, The Netherlands, Luxembourg, Spain, Portugal, Italy, Austria, Ireland, Finland, and Greece.

F

* Foreign Exchange (forex): The market in which participants are able to buy, sell, exchange, and speculate on currencies—that's money, moolah, dough, bread, cold hard cash ... get it? The forex markets is made up of banks, commercial companies, central banks, investment management firms, hedge funds, retail forex brokers, and smart investors like you.

* Fundamental Analysis: The analysis of economic indicators, political and current events that could affect the future direction of financial markets. In the foreign exchange market, fundamental analysis is based primarily on what some would call "macroeconomics," or global economic events.

H

* Hedge or Hedging: A strategy to reduce the risk of adverse price movements on your portfolio and to protect

against the volatility of the market. Hedging usually involves selling or buying at a forward-looking price or taking a position in a related security. Investors hedge more when there is increasing uncertainty about current market conditions.

L
* Limit order: An order with restrictions on the maximum price to be paid or the minimum price to be received.

* Liquidity: The ability of a market to accept large transactions with no impact on price.

M
* Margin: The percentage of the total value of a transaction that a trader must have in his or her account balance to cover the order.

* Market Order: The most popular ordering method to buy or sell a currency pair at the best available price.

O
* Offer: The price a seller is willing to accept.

* Order: A financial instruction by a customer to their broker to buy or sell at a certain price or market price. The order remains valid until executed or cancelled by the customer.

* Over-the-Counter Market: When one party trades directly with another with no exchange involved in the transaction.

P

* Pip (Points): The smallest amount an exchange rate can move, typically .0001.

Q

* Quote Currency: The second currency in a pair.

R

* Rollover: A charge or credit for holding a currency position overnight. The cost of the process is measured by the interest rate differential between the two currencies.

S

* Spot Price: The price at which commodities, securities, or currencies are immediately exchanged.

* Spread: The difference between the bid and offer price.

* Swap: The rollover credit or charge.

T

* Technical Analysis: The technique used to try to predict future movements of a security, commodity, or currency based on past price movements and volume levels. It examines charts and historical performance. Most forex robots can only use this method, while some claim to have an ability to adapt their methodology based on market news.

* Tick: A single price movement.

* Transaction Costs: The costs that are incurred by a trader when buying or selling currencies, commodities, or currencies. These costs include broker commissions or spreads.

* Transaction Date: The date when a trade occurs.

* Trend Lines: Straight lines drawn across a chart that indicate the overall trend for the currency pair. In an upward trend, the line is drawn below and acts as a support line; the opposite holds true for a downward trend. Once the currency breaks the trend line, the trend is considered to be invalid.

U
* Unidentified Forex Object (UFO): Just making sure you are paying attention. If you see one of these, run!

V
* Volume: An important indication of how strong the current trend is based upon real-time trading information. If the volume is high to sell, a related indicator will be red, while if the volume is high to buy, the indicator is usually green. Two good volume indicators are the SMA-Angle and the MAAngle.

References

Secret Forex Report (www.secretforexreport.com)

Forex Peace Army (www.forexpeacearmy.com)

Google (www.google.com)

United States Commodity Futures Trading Commission (www.cftc.gov)

National Futures Association (www.nfa.futures.org)

Wikipedia (www.wikipedia.org)

Disclaimer

Forex trading, also known as FX and as off-exchange foreign currency futures and options, involves substantial risk of loss and is not suitable for every investor. Forex is *very* risky!

All of my advice is from my own personal experience. If I make a recommendation to you, it might not work for you at all. You really have to make your own intelligent decision. Don't blame me if you lose money. I've written this book to help you know what things to do to avoid losing money. If you take a great deal of risk, there is a high probability that you will lose some or all of your investment in the forex.

The use of leverage can lead to large losses as well as gains. Under certain conditions you may find it impossible to liquidate a position. This can occur, for example, when a market becomes illiquid. The placement of contingent orders by you, such as "stop loss" or "stop limit," orders will not necessarily limit or prevent losses, because market conditions may make it impossible to execute such orders. In no event should the contents of this book or my Web site (www.secretforexreport.com) be construed as an express or implied promise or guarantee that you will profit or that losses can or will be limited in any manner whatsoever.

Currency values may fluctuate, and investors may lose all or more than their original investments. Risks also include, but are not limited to, the potential for changing economic, political, and global conditions that may substantially affect the price and liquidity of a currency. The impact of seasonal and geopolitical events is already factored into market prices.

The leveraged nature of forex trading means that any market movement will have an equally proportional effect on your deposited funds and as such may work against you as well as for you. Past results are no indication of future performance. Information contained in this correspondence is intended for informational purposes only and was obtained from sources believed to be reliable. Information is in no way guaranteed. No guarantee of any kind is implied or possible where projections of future conditions are attempted.